MILLION

DOLLAR
AUTOMOBILES

MILLION DOLLAR
DOLLAR
AUTOMOBILES

DAVID BURGESS-WISE

SPECIAL PHOTOGRAPHY BY LAURIE CADDELL

Macdonald Orbis

A *Macdonald Orbis* BOOK

© Macdonald & Co (Publishers) Ltd 1989

First published in Great Britain in 1989
by Macdonald & Co (Publishers) Ltd
London & Sydney

A member of Maxwell Pergamon Publishing Corporation plc

British Library Cataloguing in Publication Data

Burgess-Wise, David
    Million dollar automobiles.
    I. Cars, 1919–1969
    I. Title
    629.2'222'09042
    ISBN 0 356 15568 4

Typeset by Bookworm Typesetting, Manchester
Printed and bound in Spain by Cayfosa Industria
Grafica, Barcelona
Conceived and edited by CW Editorial Limited

Editor: Gillian Prince
Designers: David Goodman & Ralph Titchford
Senior art editor: Philip Lord

Macdonald & Co (Publishers) Ltd
Headway House
66–73 Shoe Lane
London EC4P 4AB

PAGE 1 The mighty Mercedes-Benz SS carried its famous three-pointed-star badge to victory in many a race. This car was once driven by Land Speed Record ace, Malcolm Campbell

PAGE 2 It was when the Ferrari 250 GT-O (the 'O' was for Omologato) was being homologated (hence the car's title) with the FIA that a typing error occurred on its papers and the hyphen was left out. Since that time, the Ferrari 'GTO' has become a legend

ACKNOWLEDGEMENTS

The author and publishers are grateful to the following for their assistance: Robert Brooks, James Allington, Victor Gauntlett, Paul Foulkes-Halbard, Ray Wiltshire, Humphrey Avon, Dennis Miller-Williams, Martin Hilton, Nicky Wright, Sophie Allington, National Motor Museum, Museo Alfa Romeo, André Sourmain, Musée National de L'Automobile, Philippe Charbonneaux's Centre Historique de L'Automobile Française, André Le Coq, Richard Freshman and Lynx Cars, Ron Hickman, Bill Medcalf, Midland Motor Museum and NASA. We are especially grateful to the Blackhawk Collection of San Ramon, California, who supplied many of the cars for photography in this book.

CONTENTS

FOREWORD 6

INTRODUCTION 7

ALFA ROMEO 8C 2300 10

ALFA ROMEO 8C 2900 18

ASTON MARTIN DBR2 26

BENTLEY SPEED SIX 34

BUCCIALI 42

BUGATTI ROYALE 50

BUGATTI TYPE 55 56

BUGATTI TYPE 57 62

CADILLAC V16 68

DELAGE D8 78

DELAHAYE TYPE 135 86

DELAHAYE TYPE 145 94

DUESENBERG MODEL J 100

FERRARI 250 SWB/GTO 110

FERRARI TESTA ROSSA 116

FORD GT40 122

HISPANO-SUIZA H6C 128

HISPANO-SUIZA V12 134

ISOTTA FRASCHINI 142

JAGUAR XK-SS 150

LUNAR ROVER 158

MAYBACH 164

MERCEDES 60 172

MERCEDES-BENZ SS 180

MERCEDES-BENZ 540K 188

MERCER 196

PACKARD V12 204

PIERCE-ARROW V12 210

ROLLS-ROYCE SILVER GHOST 218

TALBOT-LAGO 224

VOISIN V12 232

INDEX 240

FOREWORD

FOREWORD BY VICTOR GAUNTLETT, EXECUTIVE CHAIRMAN OF ASTON MARTIN LAGONDA

For many, the thought of a million dollars fires the imagination; for even more, thoughts of exclusive, potent, sporting or exotic motor cars does the same. The combination of the two is heady stuff!

I believe that when you read David Burgess-Wise's book you will be transported into a world of veritable Kings of the Road, each different one from another. Some have spectacular performance; some have spectacular coach-work; some combine the two; but all have that sheer presence born of the melding of care, craftsmanship and intellect – presence that one cannot always define, but which one can recognise as instantly in a motor car as in a man. For me that spine-tingling presence says this is a million-dollar motor car, if not today, then certainly tomorrow.

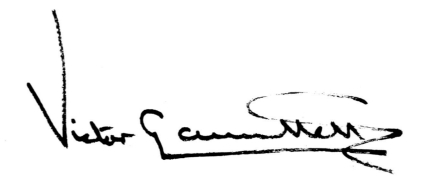

INTRODUCTION

I n the words of Sir Henry Royce, who knew more about the subject than most, 'The quality remains long after the price is forgotten. . . '.

That's still true and the important thing about any car, whatever value the world places on it, is how much pleasure you get from driving it. I've been lucky enough, in thirty years of playing with old cars, to have driven several cars that nowadays fall into the exalted million dollar bracket and I know I got just as big a thrill out of driving them when they were worth less than a new family car as I still do now that their values have soared into the stratosphere.

As an old friend of mine, who has owned some seven hundred antique cars – and sold most of them again – in his quest for automotive perfection, told me after he had refused an offer of a million pounds for two of his most treasured possessions: 'The money's not important; I'd never find those cars again!'

So it holds true for all genuine enthusiasts that if you love, you don't count the cost. However, the question still remains: how does a car enter the rare élite of the million-dollar automobile? What indefinable qualities give a car a potential seven-figure worth? It can't just be rarity: there are many cars which are rare – unique, even – which will never achieve a high value, because their rarity has nothing to do with exclusivity or quality. Conversely, some cars survive in relatively large numbers yet

The mighty Maybach Zeppelin was so large that its drivers needed an omnibus licence and it cost almost twice as much as its contemporary, the Mercedes-Benz 540K. Power was from a 7-litre V12, which despite its size still had a job propelling over 3 tons of car

they are virtually guaranteed a million-dollar price tag.

In November 1987 I was present when the world record price of £5 million ($8.9 million) was paid for one of the six extant Bugatti Royales: it took only a couple of minutes for the car to be sold, the bids leaping upwards in steps that would each have bought a fairly substantial house in the Home Counties. When the hammer finally fell, the crowd who had gathered to watch the sale in London's Albert Hall applauded enthusiastically.

Who better, I thought, to define the parameters that determine a million-dollar motor than the debonair Robert Brooks, the Christie's auctioneer who heads that august establishment's vintage car department and who conducted the sale of the Royale with such aplomb.

'It's difficult actually to pin down what it is that makes a car valuable,' admitted Robert. 'It's a combination of about a hundred and one different things, but most particularly demand in the market place. The reason that a Bugatti Royale becomes incredibly valuable is a combination of its rarity, the fact that it was built as the best of all cars and because when cars became popular collectors' items, all the Royales were found to be in permanent hands.

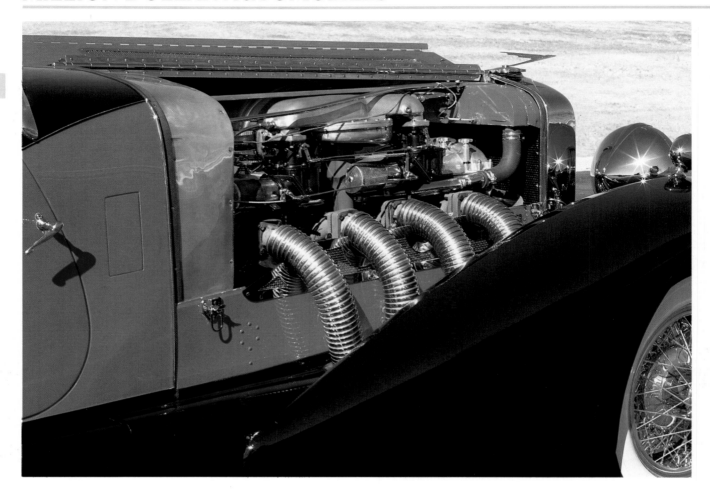

'An example of a car that has become valuable even though there is a fairly steady supply is the Duesenberg. In that particular instance, the American market has always been the largest and broadest and consequently there's always been a demand for the best of American cars.

'So it's difficult to pin down why a particular car is valuable; *how* you value it is a little easier, because it tends to be a matter of trends within a fairly broadly defined market and it's usually straightforward to predict that, for instance, a 4½-litre Bentley will be more valuable than a 3-litre Bentley, or that a V12 Hispano is going to be more valuable than a six-cylinder Hispano.

'It becomes a little bit more difficult when cars go in and out of fashion within a particular sphere. Take, for instance, the fact that GTB4 Ferraris, Tour de France Ferraris and SWB Ferraris are very fashionable, but some of the less-powerful road cars like the Lusso have only recently started to come into fashion.

'You sometimes experience swap-overs in which one car becomes more valuable than the other; a Ferrari Lusso is now nearly as valuable as a Daytona, whereas for a long time Daytonas had probably twice the value of Lussos. Again, that's simply a matter of keeping in touch

The Duesenberg SJ was the epitome of the high-performance luxury American car of the 1930s with its supercharged straight-eight engine. Before any 'Duesy' chassis was handed over to a coachbuilder, it had to complete a 500-mile test at the famous Indianapolis 'brickyard'

with trends. Once you've established what those trends are, knowing where the top end and the bottom end are is a simple question of record.

'For instance, somebody recently paid a million pounds for an 8C Alfa Romeo; that means that the ceiling for eight-cylinder Alfa Romeos has just moved up a little bit, although it won't necessarily affect the value of all 8C Alfas.

'So valuing is straightforward, to the extent of keeping in touch with the market, knowing what's going on, and being there all the time. What gives one car value over another is more difficult to discern, although when it comes to selling the very expensive cars, you generally start off knowing, within fairly broad terms, where the market is going to lie and you adjust your campaign towards that market.

'For instance, with the Royale, I knew the market was going to lie within ten or fifteen buyers, so the marketing was pitched towards them. You have, at the same time, to maintain a profile for the car, which involves a lot of hard work, publicity and promotion.'

What, I asked Robert, was it like to knock down such a car for a record price?

'For cars,' he replied, 'as with most collectable items, the selling process involves some very practical considerations and a certain amount of mystique; we sometimes don't know why somebody has gone for a particular car.

'When it actually comes to selling a car, the most intriguing part for the auctioneer is the element of the unknown right until the hammer falls; and that really is also the most exciting thing.

'The Royale, indeed, was sold to someone who didn't feature on my original list of ten or fifteen potential buyers. The eventual buyer wasn't a total surprise – he'd registered to bid, obviously – but had you asked me six weeks before the car came up for sale whether this man would buy it, I would have said: "No".'

Is the Royale's auction record impregnable? Robert Brooks thinks not: 'There are other cars which could attack the record, which fall in the £4–5–6 million bracket. Notable among the high flyers would be a German Grand Prix car like a W154 Mercedes, or the right Duesenberg – one of the short-chassis film star SS SJ cars certainly could make that kind of money.

'For unusual prices, you have to look towards cars with good background histories – racing histories and the like. The track provides a good percentage of the really valuable cars; sports-racing history is having a major influence on price and retrospective events like the Mille Miglia are making a big difference. A 450S Maserati is going to make more money than a 250F because a single-seater can only be raced infrequently, while a 450S can be used on the road – although I wouldn't like to use one there myself!'

I asked Robert about an older generation of sports-racer, like the Bentley team cars?

'The right Bentley team car is potentially worth millions, becuase it embodies everything glamorous about motor sport and the classic British car – one of the great Birkin blowers could be a phenomenal thing in the market-place; but they are in such firm long-term hands that the likelihood of that happening is remote. . . .'.

The rapid rise in value of the first-rank cars means, of course, that the values of less-exalted classic cars are sucked up in their wake: 'Ordinary 3-litre and 4½-litre Bentleys are rocketing in price – you have to pay £100 000 for the right 3-litre and £150 000 plus for the right 4½-litre. There are an awful lot of cars in the £100 000-plus bracket now – but there seems to be an

endless supply of people out there with £100 000 to spend on them!'

The seemingly unstoppable rise in value of the finest old cars, thinks Brooks, might perhaps slow a little, 'because if it continues at the same rate, pretty soon we'll be talking about £20 million motor cars. Yet who knows? It's perfectly possible: it's happened with the picture market.

'To put it into perspective: when the Bugatti Royale made £5 million, it was one of the ten most expensive

The polished splendour of a Bentley Speed Six engine. In spite of it being more powerful and smoother than its four-cylinder, 3-litre predecessors, not all were happy with it. Edwin Foden, of the famous eponymous truck company, told W.O. Bentley 'it lacks the bloody thump of the four!'

works of art ever sold at auction. One hears about £20 million-plus pictures – there have only been two; one hears about £10 million plus pictures – there have only been three – including the two £20 million pictures! It's a lot of money!

'Cars are no longer on the edge of the top end of the art market – they're right in there, alongside old master paintings, alongside impressionist paintings, alongside the rarest and most valuable medieval books. The Royale is ahead of all the furniture, all the jewellery, that has ever been sold. Whether we'll ever see the ten most expensive works of art including five or six cars is a more difficult question.

'Some people claim that if the only completely drophead Royale, the Weinberger cabriolet, were to come to auction, despite its lack of originality, then it could make somewhere between £10 million and £20 million. . . .'

ALFA ROMEO 8C 2300

It was a major coup for Enzo Ferrari (then an Alfa-Romeo team driver) when in 1923 he persuaded the brilliant designer Vittorio Jano to leave Fiat, where he was becoming increasingly frustrated by the company's refusal to give him a free hand in improving their racing cars, and join Alfa, where he was to create a new Grand Prix car for the 1924 season. The new P2 Alfa was on the drawing-board at the beginning of October 1923 and on its first starting-grid on the following 9 June, when Antonio Ascari won the 200-mile Circuit of Cremona race. It was a sensational start to the P2's racing career, which culminated in its winning the World Championship for Racing Manufacturers for Alfa in 1925.

Jano translated the lessons he had learned from racing into an outstanding series of sports cars starting with the 6C 1500 of 1925. This was followed by the 6C 1750, then, after much speculation that Alfa was developing a new sporting eight-cylinder model, Jano unveiled his *capolavoro*, the 8C 2300, in the spring of 1931.

The 2336 cc power unit of the 8C 2300 was of unusual construction, for the twin helical gear wheels which drove the twin overhead camshafts, the supercharger, the water pump and the double oil pump for the dry-sump lubrication were mounted between two main bearings at the centre of the massive crankshaft. So not only was the crankshaft made in two halves and bolted together through the central gear wheels, but the

Among the most elegant sports cars of the 1930s, the Alfa Romeo 8C 2300 was the masterpiece of one of Italy's most gifted automotive designers, Vittorio Jano. Shortly before his death in 1988, Enzo Ferrari recalled that this 1931 8C 2300MM Zagato Spider Corto was almost certainly the very car with which he concluded his racing career by winning the Bobbio-Del Penice hillclimb in 1931; the car subsequently came to England, where it was owned by the racing driver Goldie Gardner. Its present owner, Paul Foulkes-Halbard, believes that this car also won the 1933 Mille Miglia, driven by the 'Flying Mantuan', Tazio Nuvolari

Latest Series (June 1934) Alfa Romeo 8-cyl, supercharged, works prepared Le Mans 4-seater, actual car which finished 2nd at Le Mans in 1935, and has run only 12000 miles since new, capable of 120 mph and over with perfect reliability and docility in traffic, finished in azure blue with red upholstery, has just been decarbonised, rebored, and fitted with Hepolite pistons by us; an outstanding car at £575.

Monza Service Ltd advertisement, July 1938

BELOW With its elegantly finned inlet manifold and neat layout, the engine of the Alfa 8C 2300 is one of the finest-looking automotive power units of all time. The drive to the twin overhead camshafts is between the two separate cylinder blocks, giving a well balanced appearance to the unit. This particular engine has been bored out to 2.6 litres and also has magnesium cylinder blocks

cylinders were cast in two blocks of four, united by the timing gear housing, and the twin overhead camshafts were also made in two halves.

Although the prototype cylinder blocks were made of cast-iron, on production 8C 2300 Alfas the engines had alloy blocks with dry liners; the one-piece alloy cylinder heads incorporated hemispherical combustion chambers. In standard form, this power unit developed 130 bhp, but the racing Monza version

could achieve 178 bhp.

The public debut of the new car was particularly dramatic, two early 8C 2300 Alfas being entered for the Mille Miglia road race as a 'preliminary test' for the following Targa Florio. The Mille Miglia saw the new Alfa of Tazio Nuvolari only managing ninth place (there was talk of clutch problems) and its sister car, plagued by 'happenings', retiring after skidding into a wall, but the Targa Florio was a different story.

With the engine apparently bored out by an extra 2 mm to give a capacity of 2482 cc, Nuvolari's car covered the twisting 363 miles of the race at an average speed of 40.29 mph, finishing just over two minutes ahead of Umberto Borzacchini, in his six-cylinder Alfa.

The 8C 2300 Alfa was produced in two wheelbase lengths, and the long-wheelbase Le Mans four-seater version won the Le Mans 24-hour race in 1931–2–3–4. The short-wheelbase competition 2300MM (for Mille Miglia) won the 1000-mile Italian classic road race in 1932–3–4.

Indeed, the 8C 2300 was virtually invincible in sports car racing in its heyday, which lasted from 1931–34. During that period, a total of 188 8C 2300 Alfas were built; although a 2.6-litre version was never officially catalogued, several of the competition cars were bored out to give a swept volume of 2557 cc, particularly by the Scuderia Ferrari, which ran the 'works' Alfa Romeo racing team between 1929 and 1938. There was also a Grand Prix version of the 8C 2300, the Monza, which was the inspiration for the P3 single-seat racing car.

The success of the 8C 2300 line was

BELOW Balanced lines grace the Foulkes-Halbard Alfa Romeo, which in its racing days wore a third, central headlamp supported by stays from the dumb-irons to the top of the radiator shell

ABOVE LEFT & RIGHT The Cavallino Rampante insignia of the Scuderia Ferrari, proudly worn by this Alfa Romeo, was originally the crest of World War I Italian flying ace Francesco Baracca, presented to Enzo Ferrari by Baracca's family in the 1920s and first used on Scuderia Ferrari cars in 1933. The quick-fill petrol cap (*right*) is another hint of the car's competition history

not echoed in the commercial fortunes of the Alfa Romeo company, which in 1933 found itself in such dire straits that it was taken over by the Italian government, and during the remainder of the pre-war period, the sporting successes of the Milanese company were seen as a reflection of the achievements of Mussolini's Fascist regime. Indeed, on the international racing scene, Alfa Romeo enjoyed outstanding success – until the German Nazi-sponsored teams of Mercedes and Auto Union began to set the pace.

Driving the 8C 2300 Alfa is an unforgettable experience: this author has ridden round the Le Mans 24-hour circuit in the long-chassis 8C 2300 belonging to Bill Lake, which impressed not only for its speed but for its immense braking power, and he's driven the ex-Scuderia Ferrari Spider Corto belonging to Paul Foulkes-Halbard, a car brought into this country in the early 1930s and once owned by racing driver Goldie Gardner.

To switch on the engine of the 8C 2300 – Paul's car has a motor enlarged to 2600 cc, with magnesium blocks and head – you push in a hefty key that looks more suited to winding clockwork trains and then push the adjacent starter button; the engine catches with a potent roar. You let it warm up, and it responds gratifyingly as you blip the tiny central throttle pedal.

Dip the firm clutch, and push the central gear lever firmly into bottom. As the car gets under way, declutch, and gently move up into second; there's so much low-speed torque available from that lusty power unit that there's no need to over-rev, so select third, and then go on up into top.

The car moves lithely, the big Ferrari steering wheel flicking lightly in your hands – one thing you mustn't do is grip the steering hard. You feel yourself as one with the car, like some kind of motorised centaur, half man, half Alfa – few cars have ever been so much an extension of the driver's persona. . . .

Into a corner, one of those tricky bends that curls back on itself; double-declutch down into third, the big straight-cut gears snicking neatly home, and just aim the car with your eyes.... The high-geared steering is such that you almost seem to wish the car round the bend rather than physically steer it and all the time that glorious bellowing of the blown straight-eight serves as accompaniment....

Sitting where little Tazio Nuvolari, perhaps the greatest racing driver of all, once sat, you experience a little of the thrill of the 8C 2300 Alfa's finest hours, racing from city to city by day and through the night in the Mille Miglia, when drivers with muscles like whipcord washed the gritty dust of the Italian roads from their mouths with coarse red wine.

RIGHT This Alfa 8C 2300MM is in remarkably original condition and has never been restored, just kept in good order. During the 1930s, the London garage which maintained the car lent it for road test to the magazine *Motor Sport* without asking the permission of the then owner, rally driver James Wright ... and he didn't find out about the test for another 50 years!

LEFT A necessity for racing, the twin spare wheels of the Alfa are partly housed in the sloping tail of the Zagato body. Even for spirited road use, the extra tyres are essential. In the 1930s, James Wright recalls, he managed to wear out a set of tyres on a trip to Yorkshire!

ALFA ROMEO 8C 2900

With the cold wind nagging round the windscreen at my cheek, we accelerated to 65 mph in second, 90 mph in third and to 110 mph (4500 rpm) in top on the Denham by-pass past London Film Productions' studios. The car was still accelerating when Hunter braked for the gradual curve which followed. . . .

John Dugdale, testing Hugh Hunter's 2.9-litre Alfa Romeo, 1939

ABOVE & RIGHT One of the most unconventional versions of the Alfa 8C 2900 was this aerodynamic coupé built for the 1938 24 Heures du Mans and driven by Raymond 'Coeur du Lion' Sommer and Clemente Biondetti. It was the fastest car in the race, and lapped at over 96 mph. It was leading by 115 miles from the second-place Delahaye when a tyre burst, damaging the bodywork. Shortly afterwards, a broken valve put the car out of the race

Alfa Romeo's golden days seemed to be over when the ailing company came under the control of the state industrial group IRI in 1933, and the purse-strings were snapped shut.

The charismatic 8C 2300 was replaced by a more prosaic – but more profitable – twin-cam six, the 6C 2300. The Scuderia Ferrari did race examples of the 6C 2300 and a small run of a sporting variant called the Pescara was built, but the new 2.3-litre Alfas paled into insignificance when compared with their eight-cylinder predecessor.

It wasn't until 1936 that Alfa redressed the situation with the launch of an even faster, even rarer, twin-cam eight-cylinder car, the twin-supercharger 8C 2900.

Indeed, the first series of the new 2.9-litre Alfas – Tipo 8C 2900A – was not even destined for sale to the public and just eleven of these cars were built; they were a sports-racing version of the Alfa Romeo Tipo B Grand Prix car, a Tipo B fitted with road equipment having won the 1935 Mille Miglia, driven by Carlo Pintacuda.

The Tipo 8C 2900A had a 170 bhp engine in a 9 ft-wheelbase chassis, with all-round independent suspension, and weighed a mere 1650 lb. Campaigned during 1936 by the Scuderia Ferrari, the model took the first three places in that year's Mille Miglia and also won the 24-hour race at Spa in Belgium.

Late in 1937, the 8C 2900B appeared, its 2.9-litre supercharged engine taken from the surplus factory stock of Tipo B Grand Prix power units remaining after the Alfa Romeo works had ceased to campaign the no-longer-competitive Tipo B. There were thirty-two of these units, so the production run was perforce limited to thirty cars, although – remarkably – the 8C 2900B was available in two chassis lengths.

The chassis itself was derived from that

of the 6C 2300B, but it was much stiffened and equipped with trailing-link front suspension and rear swing axles controlled by a transverse leaf spring, a combination which gave 'superlatively high' standards of road-holding.

Recalled Anthony Crook, who owned one of only two short-chassis 8C 2900B Alfas imported into Britain: 'The suspension . . . is truly remarkable, being far in advance of anything I have yet been fortunate enough to sample. Cornering can be effected at fantastic speeds, and

ABOVE One of the usual complaints about early aerodynamic bodywork was that access to the engine was difficult, but the unorthodox design of the Le Mans Alfa 8C 2900B could hardly be bettered for accessibility, a hatch in the full-width wing laying the entire side of the engine open to inspection

BELOW The interior
appointments of the Alfa
8C 2900B may be spartan by
modern-day standards, but
compared with contemporary
sports racers they were
positively sybaritic. Adherence
to the aerodynamic theories
of former Zeppelin designer
Paul Jaray, with the tapering
plan form of the passenger
compartment, made the Alfa
very definitely a two-
seater car

the suspension is at once comfortable, yet
not sloppy. So secure does the car feel at
100 mph or so that those who have
passengered in it believed the speed to be
much less'.

The power of the engine – between
180 and 200 bhp – was transmitted to the
four-speed transmission (built in unit with
the final drive) through a notably fierce
multi-plate clutch and, since the car
weighed only 24 cwt, ready for the road,
acceleration was summarised by Crook as
'phenomenal . . . hit-in-the-back . . . slightly
terrific from 100 mph onwards!'. On this

note, Alfa issued new owners of the 8C
2900B with running-in instructions urging
them not to exceed 90 mph for the first
950 miles. . . .

In 1938, 8C 2900B Alfas won the Spa
24-hour race and took the first three
places in the Mille Miglia, while an
aerodynamic coupé entered for Le Mans
proved to be the fastest car in the race,
capable of lapping at over 96 mph.

This car – which still exists – was
leading by the phenomenal margin of 115
miles after 18 hours, when a tyre burst on
the three-mile Mulsanne Straight,
damaging the bodywork. Soon
afterwards, the car retired.

The 1938 Mille Miglia winner was sent
to London at the time of that year's
Motor Show to promote the 'production'
8C 2900, which sold in Britain for £1950
on the short chassis, £2050 on the long,
prices equivalent to some £50 000 in
1988 terms. The car was imported into
England on the strict understanding that it
was to be returned to the factory after
the show, but racing driver Hugh Hunter
managed to persuade Alfa to sell it to him,
for it seemed to him to combine the ideal
– a car that could be both raced and used
on the roads without the need for
periodic rebuilds.

Although journalist Dennis May wrote
of the bucket seats seeming to 'enfold you
with a benevolent tyranny of comfort', as
a touring car the 8C 2900B had certain
defects: the weather equipment was
restricted to a scanty pair of aeroscreens
and, the long tail being filled with tankage
for 38 gallons of fuel and 5 gallons of oil
for the dry-sump lubrication system,
there was no luggage accommodation.
The latter, considered May, might logically
restrict teeth-cleaning to 1000-mile
intervals. . . .

Hunter had a full-width windscreen,
extra road lamps and a removeable hood
fitted, and proceeded to cram twelve
speed events into the short 1939 season
as well as covering 4500 miles on the
road. He crowned that curtailed sporting

PREVIOUS PAGE & BELOW The lines of the Alfa 8C 2900B built for the 1938 Le Mans race still seem advanced, yet they are very much of their time, an era during which automotive designers first began making use of the lessons learned in the wind tunnels built for the aviation industry

year with the 'fastest sports car' race, at Brooklands. The synchromesh gearbox gave trouble during the day, and although the Alfa won the first heat of the contest, overall victory was eventually taken by Arthur Dobson driving Rob Walker's 4.5-litre Delahaye.

The concensus of opinion was, nevertheless, that the 8C 2900 Alfa was

the fastest production sports car on the roads of the 1930s. With its high-ratio final-drive gearing installed, Hudson's car was said to be capable of exceeding 140 mph. Certainly it covered two flying laps at Brooklands at 122.97 mph in August 1939, having made a standing lap of 102.69 mph.

Even greater things were expected of

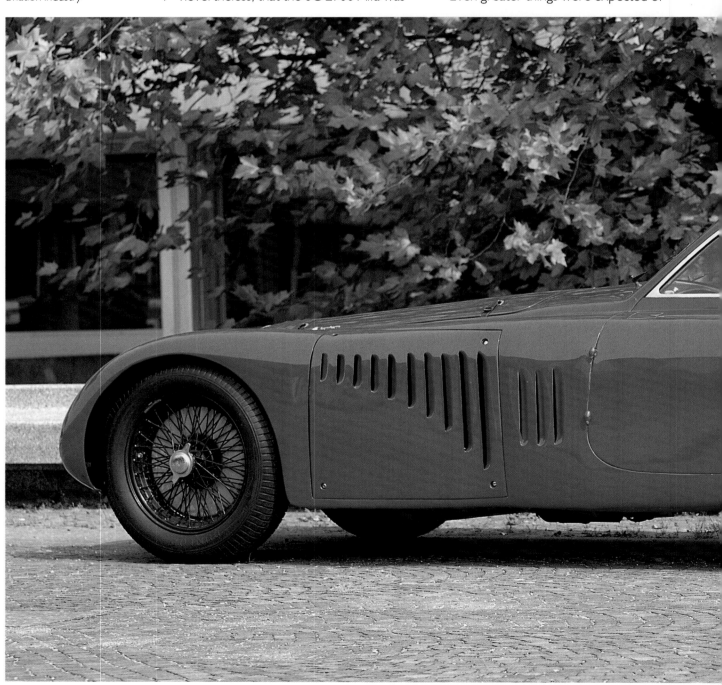

the planned successor to the 2.9 Alfa, the 1939 Tipo 412, whose 4.5-litre V12 power unit was a detuned version of that fitted to the 1937 12C–37 Grand Prix car, Jano's last design for Alfa before he was retired as 'too old' at the end of 1937.

The highly promising Tipo 412, which used the same chassis design as the 8C 2900B and strongly resembled the Mille Miglia version of that car, was never fully developed due to the war.

A hint of what might have been was given when two works Tipo 412 Alfas, driven by 'Nino' Farina and Raymond Sommer, came first and second in the 1939 Antwerp Grand Prix, easily beating their French opposition in this 190-mile sports car race.

ASTON MARTIN DBR2

Photographed outside the Newport Pagnell headquarters of Aston Martin Lagonda, DBR2/2 is the property of Aston's executive chairman Victor Gauntlett, who acquired it in 1987 and reckons that it is the best car he has ever possessed. Since Victor has owned a wide range of desirable cars, including vintage Bentleys from the 3-litre to the 4.5-litre Blower and the Speed Six, Ferraris, Jaguars and 'Olga', the prototype Bentley Continental, this is praise indeed!

The Aston Martin DBR2 is proof that the proverbial bitza can be a thoroughbred of the first water, for the two DBR2 sports racers were created in the space of a few weeks in the crowded Feltham workshops of Aston Martin Lagonda to provide mobile testbeds for the new 3.7-litre straight-six DB4 engine which had just been created by their brilliant engine designer Tadek Marek.

To do the job in the quickest possible time in readiness for the 1957 racing season, Aston's chief racing designer Ted Cutting used a couple of spaceframe chassis that were lying about the workshop, relics of an unsuccessful V12 Lagonda racer of 1955; or as the press publicity had it at the time, 'The engine and chassis are new, but the frame is a direct development of that used on the twelve-cylinder Lagonda when it appeared in prototype form at Le Mans in 1955...'. Cutting also used the gearbox, rear axle and front suspension and steering from the Lagonda, employed disc brakes all round and clothed the whole in a purposefully sleek racing body derived from that of his 1956 DBR1, which he – without any previous styling experience – had designed. Lithe and muscular, the DBR2 looks the expression of all that was best about British sports racers of the 1950s. Victor Gauntlett, who owns DBR2/2, has no doubts about its visual appeal: 'The styling is absolutely wonderful; so well formed and so balanced. There's a little game I enjoy playing when the car's down at our London showrooms; putting it on the lift and lowering it. It's absolutely wonderful to look down on as well as to look straight at and look up at. It hasn't got a wrong angle – it's that good in my

opinion – it's absolutely spectacular!'

The début of the DBR2 was not so spectacular, however; it ran alongside the DBR1s at Le Mans in June 1957, driven by the Whitehead brothers, Graham and Peter. During practice, they realised what an exceptionally quick car they had, so they kept the speed down along the Mulsanne straight in case team manager John Wyer took the Aston away from

We had these chassis standing about, so I started building a car, almost out of the parts bins.

Ted Cutting, designer

them and gave it to Tony Brooks or Roy Salvadori, the top works drivers. In the race, however, the DBR2 suffered from fuel starvation, which prevented it from realising its potential. Then an oil breather on the gearbox became blocked, all the oil was pumped out and the transmission failed. The Whiteheads were convinced that with a proper fuel system the DBR2 could have won.

Roy Salvadori demonstrated the potential of the DBR2 at Silverstone later in that year by defeating the Aston marque's biggest rival in short-distance events, Archie Scott-Brown's Lister-Jaguar. During the next year, Stirling Moss won the sports car race at the Easter Goodwood meeting and the British Empire Trophy at Oulton Park with the DBR2, now fitted with a 3.9-litre power unit; but the regulation for international sports car events had changed, restricting maximum capacity to 3 litres, so the European racing life of the DBR2 was

short. That life closed with a second place in the Spa Sports Car Grand Prix for the Belgian driver Paul Frère in May 1957, and thereafter both DBR2s were shipped to America, where they had a long racing career, with Stirling Moss achieving the last-ever victory for a works-entered open Aston Martin at the Nassau, Bahamas, sports car race late in 1959.

DBR2/1 was eventually acquired by Victor Gauntlett's American partner, Peter Livanos, and its impeccable road performance whetted Victor's appetite for owning the second car, which seemed firmly ensconced in a private collection. A chance encounter with a friend in Geneva Airport early in 1987 brought the amazing news that the owner of DBR2/2 was considering selling his car. Recalls Gauntlett: 'I was on the phone so bloody fast – this was a Sunday, in fact – and on the Monday I managed to do the deal over the phone; I was so overjoyed! Peter Livanos bolstered my morale, for it was as

FAR LEFT & LEFT Housed in a space-frame chassis originally designed for an unsuccessful Lagonda racing car, the Aston Martin DBR2 sports racer was intended as a rolling testbed for the new Tadek Marek-designed Aston straight-six power unit that was to go into production in the DB4. Because of the width of the Lagonda chassis, the cockpit space is unusually generous

BOTH PAGES Considering its mongrel origins, the Aston DBR2 has remarkable detail finish, from the neat gear-change gate (*right*) – the wide transmission tunnel was one of the problems with the Lagonda space-frame chassis design – to the trilobate hub nuts (*far right, above*) and the smooth nasal contours of the two-seater bodywork (*far right, below*). 'It hasn't got a wrong angle,' says Victor Gauntlett

much money as I'd ever paid for a motor car, that's for sure! It seemed a hell of a lot of money at the time – it seems quite reasonable now! I was so excited to get hold of it.

'The DBR2 is without doubt the best car I have ever owned. It's given me more enjoyment in a shorter space of time than any other motor car!'

Gauntlett's opinion is founded on the ownership of a wide spectrum of classic cars, ranging from vintage Bentleys to Ferraris, so it is interesting to discover what are the particular features that endear the DBR2 to him.

'It starts from the outside with that spectacular styling, but a very personal facet is that I'm a big chap: it's nice to be in a motor car that's not made for midgets. There's plenty of room, it's very comfortable. . . . I once had the horror of owning a C-type Jaguar which I couldn't actually drive; there wasn't room – I was wedged between the pedals and the steering wheel! With a DBR2 one's extremely comfortable, and I think that's an important part of motoring when you're enjoying something that's potentially quick – and it is *very* quick!

'I've had the car out once or twice with a Vantage Zagato and the person in the

Vantage has had to work because the acceleration and roadholding of the DBR2 are superb. The thing that really surprises a lot of the people who drive it is the braking, which is absolutely fantastic – for that era.

'It's a very easy car to drive, very forgiving, which I always think of as a strong Aston trait; that's one of the nice things about Astons, that they aren't there to catch you out and expose you as the mediocre driver you might be – they are there actually to be friendly, to help you, to warn you, and not to drop you in it. . . . That's very important in the tradition of the cars – that's how they are. A lot of other cars may generate excitement, but they can be more treacherous. . . . In terms of enjoyment – especially enjoyment on the road, which is a very important aspect of it to me – the DBR2 is paramount.

'Frankly, after a DBR2 I believe you're struggling a bit because why do you need a Jaguar D or C or even an Aston DB3S when the DBR2 really does it all – and better! One of the reasons why I love these motor cars is that they are road-usable. To me the whole essence of the motoring that I like is the simple fact that people used to bomb off to Le Mans in cars like this, race them and, if they were lucky, drive them home afterwards. It is a proper sports car, not some sort of a pastiche of a sports car.'

There's an added bonus for Gauntlett in that the golden age of Aston Martin – the decade of the marque's only Le Mans win, by a DBR1 in 1959 (Gauntlett once owned the winning car) – is recent enough for most of the leading characters still to be around: 'How super to be able to talk to John Wyer, Ted Cutting. . . . Let's face it, there are a lot of lessons that go on and on being valid and if you're not conscious of history and of the people who've done it before, you can really waste a lot of time and money relearning those lessons. It is good to be able to talk to the drivers as well: Moss, Salvadori, Fairman, Thompson. . . .'

Gauntlett has now competed in the Mille Miglia retrospective with both

BOTH PAGES Lithe and well balanced in appearance, Gauntlett's Aston DBR2 epitomizes all that is best about the British sports racing cars of the 1950s, in an era when cars would be driven to an event like the Le Mans 24 Hours race and then – provided they had been neither bent nor broken – driven home again. . . . 'In terms of enjoyment on the road, the DBR2 is paramount,' says Gauntlett

DBR2s – he drove Livanos's DBR2/1 in 1987 and his first Mille Miglia with his own car was the 1988 event, both times with Prince Michael of Kent as co-driver, but competing in such a high-speed event on public roads in such a valuable car does not seem to worry him.

'I think the way Prince Michael and I have attacked the Mille Miglia in the past two years could reasonably be described as flat out, but one must not allow the sums of money to spoil one's enjoyment; it would be too easy to get besotted by the amount of money. If you've got a car that's worth a million pounds, you can't really do a million pounds's worth of damage. You're going to be a really unlucky person to do more than £100 000-worth; well, that already could be painful, but it puts it in perspective.

'I have a horror of people buying wonderful paintings and consigning them to a bank vault. How on earth can a painting have a value if you can't look at it and enjoy what it has to offer? In the same way, if you lock up a motor car in a museum, like a specimen pinned out on a table, what value does it have? The value has to be in the enjoyment – in the conjuring up of a different era that comes from driving it, whether it's fifty years, a hundred years or twenty years ago. That's what it's about!'

ALL VISITORS PLEASE
REPORT TO
SALES SERVICE
RECEPTION OPPOSITE

BENTLEY SPEED SIX

It was a Bentley victory so sweeping and monotonous that it became almost exciting. I have nearly a hundred press cuttings about it, and can find no comparison except the Aga Khan's recent conquest of Doncaster and the National Party triumph in the last election. Such unique success was a marvel to those that partook of it, and lasting proof that, whatever the future has in store, for a while, at least, British racing cars have been the world's champions in these events.

Sir H.R.S. 'Tim' Birkin, 1932

No-one who watched the 1988 Le Mans 24-hour race will forget the beautifully stage-managed finish, where three Jaguars crossed the line together, bringing the Coventry marque its first Le Mans victory since the great days of the 1950s. It didn't matter that only one of the cars was actually in contention, the other two being too far behind on laps covered to count; it was great motor racing theatre.

Just imagine, then, the excitement caused when, at Le Mans, 1929, the British Bentley team was so far ahead of its opposition that in the closing stages of the race the four surviving Bentleys had time to pull into the side on the Mulsanne Straight and discuss the order in which they should cross the line.... This enabled 'Babe' Barnato/Tim Birkin's 6.5-litre and the 4.5-litre of Jack Dunfee/Glen Kidston to cross the line together to receive the yellow flag that marked the finish of the race, followed a few seconds later by the two remaining 4.5-litres, driven by Dr Dudley Benjafield/Baron Leo d'Erlanger and Frank Clement/Jean Chassagne. The winning car's average speed (73.63 mph) was the fastest Le Mans victory of the 1920s, it was the first time that a British car had won the coveted Rudge-Whitworth Cup for a repeated victory at Le Mans, and the first time that a single make had taken the first four places in the race.

Bentley had won at Le Mans before, in 1924, '27 and '28, and would win again in

Archetype of the British vintage sports car, the Speed Six Bentley was also a car of great refinement which possessed remarkable performance for its day. Built in an era when the blanket speed limit in Britain was a niggardly 20 mph – a barrier erected as far back as 1904 – the Speed Six was capable of sustained cruising at speeds in excess of 90 mph on the arrow-straight roads of the Continent

BELOW & RIGHT Patrician prow of a widely travelled 1930 Speed Six Bentley: the winged 'B' badge of the Bentley marque was designed by *Autocar* artist Frederick Gordon Crosby, also responsible for the leaping jaguar mascot of the Jaguar car. But the Bentley badge first appeared on the front of a toy car that Crosby built for his young son Peter, before W.O. Bentley got his machines into production in 1919

1930, but that spectacular 1929 victory was the peak of the Cricklewood marque's sporting achievement, which had started in 1923 with a private entry of a 3-litre Bentley by the gangling John Duff, son of a missionary on the China station. Duff made fastest lap before a stone holed his petrol tank and time was lost repairing it, but he came back the following year – and won. The legend of the British at Le Mans was established.

It must be said that when W.O. Bentley, engineer and former motor agent, started to manufacture a car bearing his own name in 1919, after a distinguished wartime career designing rotary engines for the front-line fighters of the Royal Flying Corps, winning international endurance races was not a priority. His intention was to build a fast touring car of the highest quality, but the Le Mans 24-hour race seemed to fit naturally into this pattern for the Bentley, whose overhead-camshaft engine was of a type seen only on racing cars before the war. When in 1927 journalist S.C.H. 'Sammy' Davis and Harley Street specialist Dr Dudley Benjafield extracted their shattered 3-litre from a multiple pile-up in the small hours and went on to drive it to victory, the name of Bentley joined the immortals of motoring.

Because Bentley gained such international fame from its achievements on the track, the cars which are most highly prized today are the team cars, the 3, 4.5 and 6.5-litre Bentleys which ran at Le Mans and at tracks such as Brooklands; although W.O. Bentley was disdainful of them in their day, the big supercharged

4.5-litre cars converted out at Welwyn Garden City by Amherst Villiers for Sir Henry 'Tim' Birkin, whose racing efforts were backed by the massively rich Hon Dorothy Paget, are also coveted.

To appreciate the significance of the Bentley victories at Le Mans, in a race designed to produce a better breed of touring car, you really need to make a few fast laps of the 24-hour race circuit at the wheel of a vintage Bentley. This, however, is a privilege nowadays accorded to few, for although much of the race takes place on specially closed public roads, that section of the *Circuit Permanent de la Sarthe* that encompasses the pit and grandstand area is not accessible to private vehicles. In 1986, the writer was fortunate enough to drive a 3-litre Bentley in the historic parade that precedes each June's race, and in doing so became probably the first journalist to drive such a car around the circuit on race day since Sammy Davis, then sports editor of *The Autocar*, had urged the battered *Old Number Seven* to victory almost sixty years earlier.

If the 1925 Bentley handbook is to be believed: 'The Three-Litre Bentley is remarkable in that, although it is a very fast car, it is extremely easy to handle and drive. Even the inexperienced driver will soon find himself at ease when he takes the wheel, owing to the flexibility of the engine, the lightness of the steering and the efficiency of the brakes. It should, however, be realised that the speed of the Bentley is very deceptive, and at first a close watch should be kept on the speedometer.'

It was with caution in mind, therefore, that the author depressed the starter button, ignition retarded on the twin magnetos by the lever at the centre of the steering wheel; the twin SUs inhaled deeply and the engine burbled into life with a sound that was pure undiluted nostalgia. The cone clutch was moderately heavy, but for someone who had learned to drive on a car with centre

throttle, right-hand gearchange and cone clutch there was nothing strange about the Bentley's control layout.

On that 8.4-mile circuit – shorter by 2 miles, less a hairpin bend, wider and better surfaced than in the 1920s – even at parade speeds of 70 mph or so, you get something of the flavour of driving a Bentley in the 24-hour race ... the monotonously long Mulsanne straight with

LEFT & ABOVE Ergonomics were scarcely a consideration to the engineer who laid out the Bentley's dashboard, but for sheer clarity, the instrumentation could hardly be bettered. The rev-counter, which enabled the driver to monitor the engine speed, was placed more readily in view than the speedometer, since at the wheel of such a car as the Bentley it was self evident that the driver would be travelling at a speed in excess of the legal limit most of the time ...

Like so many vintage Bentleys, this car wears Van den Plas Le Mans-style fabric tourer bodywork, but the fact of the matter is that many Bentleys were originally built with more prosaic tourer, saloon or coupé coachwork and have subsequently been fitted with sporting bodies. This fashion began in the 1930s when, after the demise of the original Bentley company, W.O.'s brother H.M. Bentley began converting and updating 'proper' Bentleys for the well heeled sportsmen of the day

its famous kink and the Restaurant des Hunaudières, favoured vantage-point since 1923 . . . the sudden right-hand bend at the end of the straight . . . brake, into neutral, blip the brass throttle pedal, slip the lever into third and round . . . like most crash boxes with generously toothed gears, the change down is easy if you judge it right. . . . Bentley steering, despite the handbook's boast, *is* heavy, and you need to sit close to the wheel to get sufficient leverage on such a sharp bend . . . accelerate away and back into top and through the woods down to Indianapolis, so-called because it used to be paved with bricks from the Indy Brickyard . . . out, change up . . . then down again into third for the sharp right-hander at Arnage . . . a mile or so along is White House where the 1927 crash took place, unrecognisable now that the circuit is wide and well surfaced; they must have been supermen to race for 24 hours when this circuit was just a loose-surfaced rural track. . . .

Four laps of Le Mans is over 30 miles — back in 1924, on a slightly longer circuit that actually ran into the outskirts of Le Mans, the winning team of Duff and Clement circled the triangular course 120 times, clocking up almost 1291 miles in the process, and proving that Britain could build sports cars that were more than a match for the best the Continentals could produce. Today, your wrists and ankles ache from the effort after a simple four-lap parade. . . .

As that great amateur racing driver Humphrey Cook said, back in the 1960s, 'The Bentley was heavy compared with the cars we know today, but it was a very nice car, very well made'.

The 6.5-litre six of 1925 was the first new model to be introduced after the 3-litre, but when one of Bentley's keenest customers, the steam-wagon builder Foden, told 'W.O.' that his new six lacked the 'bloody thump' of the 3-litre four, a bigger four-cylinder model, the 4.5-litre, was launched in 1927. This went on to

win Le Mans in 1928 — with a broken chassis frame and an empty radiator. Then it was the turn of the Speed Six to win in 1929 and 1930.

The legend of superhuman effort culminated in the supercharged 4 5-litre Bentley, even though Bentley himself thought that supercharging corrupted his design. Bentley's principal backer, diamond merchant and amateur racing driver Woolf 'Babe' Barnato, liked the 'Blower Bentley' and designed his own three-seat coachwork to be built by Gurney Nutting for his personal Blower.

'I had a run in this car soon after it was completed', recalled A.F. Rivers Fletcher, 'and it certainly had tremendous punch but was inclined to boil in traffic.' Barnato recommended a reduction in compression ratio, and the car was

transformed: 'The speedometer went right round to 105 on top gear and 85 and 70 were obtained on third and second, respectively'.

Road testers admired the Blower's 'immense power, linked with great docility', but perhaps the Blower's greatest hour was in the 1930 French Grand Prix, where Tim Birkin, whose Blower 4.5, despite towering above the Bugattis, Peugeots and Delages of the other competitors, came in second, only three minutes behind 'Phi-Phi' Etancelin's Bugatti after 246 miles.

It's probably no exaggeration to say that the never-say-die spirit of the Bentley Boys, who raced and defeated the best that the Continent had to offer in the short, eleven-year, lifespan of the original Bentley company (it went under in the Depression and was taken over by Rolls-Royce) was reflected in the daring of those few young men who turned the tide of German air power in the Battle of Britain. For many of them their first glimpse of heroism had been the slight figure of Tim Birkin, polka-dot neckerchief a-flutter, at the wheel of a great green Bentley. . . .

OVERLEAF One of the most famous of all the racing Blower 4.5-litre Bentleys was this car, built as a single-seater to be raced on the banked Outer Circuit of the Brooklands race track by 'Tim' Birkin. It was fitted with this two-seater body for road use, but its racing single-seater body was found in a field, restored and reunited with the original chassis, in which form it is raced today by master horologist George Daniels

BUCCIALI

Even in the marque's brief heyday, few people can have seen a Bucciali car: the Bucciali brothers, two of life's supreme optimists, boasted of a total production of thirty-eight chassis between 1926 and 1932. The reality seems to have been less than half that number; Bucciali experts cannot agree whether this most esoteric of French manufacturers built fourteen or seventeen cars in all.

The Bucciali combined supreme rarity with exotic good looks and an adventurous specification, but sadly the dramatic statement made by these stunning-looking cars was in the eye of the beholder only. The former owner of one of the three surviving Buccialis dismissed his car as 'a low-powered nail on the road'.

The Bucciali brothers, Angelo and Paul-Albert, were Frenchmen of Corsican extraction. Their grandfather had been a noted builder of pipe organs, while their father, cursed with failing eyesight, had become a virtuoso organist. The brothers, dapper, bespectacled little men who bore an uncanny resemblance to British farce actor Robertson Hare, were trained in the family tradition, but in 1909 they took up the new sport of flying; Paul-Albert became a stunt pilot, then flew with France's premier fighter

BELOW Front-wheel drive made the Bucciali particularly low for its day, and the styling of the car, with its low-set headlamps, was as avant-garde as its specification

squadron, the *Escadrille Cicogne*, during World War I – or, at least, that's what he subsequently claimed....

With the war over, Paul-Albert turned, like so many young Frenchmen, to the fabrication of motor cars, in this case little sporting cyclecars sold under the name Buc. The first Bucs had twin-cylinder two-stroke engines of 1340 cc, but then in 1925 came a larger car with a more conventional 1600 cc four-cylinder power unit supplied by the SCAP company. Altogether, the Buc factory in Courbevoie, a north-eastern suburb of Paris, built maybe 120 cars between 1920 and 1926 – hardly a runaway commercial success.

Then the Bucciali brothers began to step outside the bounds of reality: having discovered the new technology of front-wheel drive, they collaborated with a mysterious Brazilian engineer of Franco/Russian/Spanish extraction, named Sensaud de Lavaud, to produce their first car to bear the full Bucciali name. Bucciali spoke expansively of a choice of 1.7-litre four- or 1927 cc eight-cylinder engines and six- and eight-cylinder models 'incorporating the latest progress in racing-car technology'. They built a prototype Bucciali TAV1 (for *Traction Avant* – front-wheel drive) whose advanced specification included a De Lavaud automatic transmission, electric front brakes and servo-assisted hydraulic rears and all-round independent suspension by rubber pads in compression. Fortunately for any prospective client worried about all this complexity going wrong, the Bucciali TAV1 was incapable of running – although it did cause a fine stir at the 1926 Paris Salon.

Bucciali had now entered into a peculiarly French shadow-land, inhabited by a coterie of inventors who regularly showed cars of improbably advanced specification at the annual Paris Salon in the hope of selling production licences to rich manufacturers. There were enough

Only one sixteen-cylinder car is to be found in the Show, this being the Bucciali, built by a firm apparently more interested in selling licences than in producing cars in quantities.
The Autocar, 1930

of these – they also included the makers of the Claveau, the Harris-Léon Laisne, and Dubonnet – to cause the press to complain that such cars were stealing space in the crowded Grand Palais, where the Salon was held, from 'fully established firms'. Elaborate catalogues were produced and extravagant claims made, but Bucciali sales were remarkable by their absence.

Two more Bucciali cars appeared at the 1927 Paris Salon, a development of the 1926 model and thus known as TAV2. One of them was fitted with a prosaic 2442 cc American side-valve six built by Continental, erstwhile supplier of engines to Morris, but it's doubtful whether either TAV2 – one had Sensaud de Lavaud rubber suspension, the other quarter-elliptic leaf springs – was capable of locomotion.

A year later, a third Bucciali design appeared, known variously as TAV6, from the number of cylinders in its

ABOVE The square-cut radiator of the Bucciali was reminiscent of that of one of the leading American marques, the air-cooled Franklin, perhaps with the US market in mind

OVERLEAF The body fitted to the Blackhawk Collection's Bucciali TAV8 is by that master of bizarre styling, Jacques Saoutchik, the Russian-born furniture designer turned society *carrossier* – but it's not original to this chassis, which once wore crude four-seated tourer coachwork

ABOVE The power unit of the extravagant Bucciali TAV8 was far from exotic, for it was a prosaic 4.4-litre side-valve American Continental engine, built by a company that had once supplied engines for the Bullnose Morris Cowley

Continental engine, or TAV15, from its taxable horsepower rating. It was possibly a scissors-and-paste amalgamation of the 1926 and 1927 cars, and *The Autocar* found it 'rather complicated-looking (but) not extremely impressive', although with its low-slung construction and massive cast-aluminium wheels carrying tyres with an outside diameter of 3 ft, the new Bucciali was certainly different.

It is claimed that three functional TAV6 cars were built and sold in 1929–30. Those poor little Continental sixes must have had a hard time stirring the hefty Buccialis into action, particularly since all were reportedly fitted with solidly built close-coupled four-seat *faux cabriolet* coachwork designed by the brothers Bucciali.

The shortcomings in the propulsive department were corrected in the TAV8, which first appeared in prototype form in mid 1929 and was powered by a

Continental straight-eight – still with side valves – which displaced some 4.4 litres. There was talk of a variant with a 3921 cc supercharged Mercedes six, but, like so many of the Buccialis' schemes, it was pure fantasy. Nevertheless, the TAV8 attracted the attention of an American entrepreneur named Coldwell Johnson, who represented E.L. Cord's interests in Europe and was not averse to lining his own pockets when the occasion arose. He took the American rights to the Johnson-Bucciali Front Wheel Drive System and shipped the 1929 Paris Salon TAV8, hastily fitted with a four-seat-tourer body, to New York as an unofficial adjunct to the January 1930 Motor Show. Johnson, stoutly-built and moustachioed, physically resembled Oliver Hardy while the Buccialis, who accompanied him across the Atlantic, looked like twin Laurels.

Front-wheel drive was heralded as the

coming thing at the New York Show, with cars using this system from Cord, Ruxton and Gardner on display, but the only interest that Johnson could raise came from Peerless of Cleveland, a once-great car manufacturer that had fallen on hard times.

In October that year, Bucciali announced that Peerless had taken up the American rights to their transmission and would produce a front-wheel-drive car in the near future. In return, Bucciali took on European sales for Peerless and rented a showroom in the Champs-Elysées whose fascia bore the Bucciali name in frivolously embellished art deco lettering. Nothing came of the Peerless connection, for that company ceased production in June 1931, closed its works for two years and then, with the ending of prohibition, re-emerged not as a maker of luxury cars, but as the brewer of Carling's Ale. . . .

Bucciali, meanwhile, was engaged on its most bizarre flight of fancy, the Double-Huit sixteen-cylinder model, whose engine appeared at first glance to be made up of two straight-eights mounted in parallel, with their crankshafts geared together. 'This is incorrect, however,' admonished *The Autocar*, 'for although the two aluminium cylinder blocks are vertical, with a few inches between them, the cylinder barrels are at 22 degrees, and there is only one five-bearing crankshaft, which can be dropped from below without taking the engine out of the frame.' Twin radiators were fitted, one ahead of the front-wheel drive housing, one behind, and it was claimed that the wet-liner engine displaced 7.8 litres.

The Double-Huit appeared at the Paris Salons of 1930, '31 and '32 in chassis form (the Bucciali brothers claimed that there was a different chassis each year) to the admiration of all who beheld it; miraculously, it survived the War, and was for many years in the collection of Serge Pozzoli, stored beneath the concrete banking of the Montlhéry race circuit.

Eventually, it became one of the 1200-

ABOVE & LEFT To divert attention from the humble origins of the TAV8's engine, the Bucciali brothers paid meticulous attention to dressing-up the Plain-Jane power unit with polished aluminium castings and plates which gave it at least the semblance of custom construction

odd vehicles owned by gambling millionaire William Harrah, of Reno, Nevada, who resolved to put the mysterious V16 engine into running order. Harrah ordered his workshop to strip the engine down, but that glorious light-alloy unit turned out to contain not one, nor even two, crankshafts, but only old French newspapers.

Bucciali built further front-wheel-drive cars. The TAV30, with a 5.2-litre Lycoming straight-eight, was based on the TAV8, and a few of these were built and ran successfully, while the TAV12, which used the complex V12 sleeve-valve engine of the Voisin car, was one of the more stunning exhibits at the 1932 Paris Salon, the stork emblem of the *Escadrille Cicogne* appearing on the bonnet sides of this super-low coupé styled by the most daring of French coachbuilders, Jacques Saoutchik. Like the Double Huit and a lone TAV8, the TAV12 is in California.

It seems perhaps appropriate that the state that gave birth to Hollywood today houses these larger than life motor cars, whose bizarre lines have so excited

enthusiasts that in recent years two Bucciali 'look-alikes' have been built, regardless of cost, by enthusiasts who despaired of ever acquiring the real thing. And those two cars almost certainly run far better than ever the real thing did.

LEFT The flying-stork emblem on the bonnet sides of the Bucciali recalls Paul-Albert Bucciali's claim to have flown with France's crack World War I fighter squadron, the *Escadrille Cicogne*, whose crest also inspired the emblems of the Hispano-Suiza and Bignan marques

BUGATTI ROYALE

Early this summer a new type Bugatti, which can certainly claim to be the biggest private car in the world, and also the most expensive, for the chassis price will be half a million francs, or slightly more than £4000, is expected to make its appearance.

W.F. Bradley, 1927

It seems odd that Ettore Bugatti, who made his name building cars of the most delicate appearance and sarcastically congratulated W.O. Bentley on building the fastest lorries in the world, should have created a car which for sheer size and weight was itself actually larger than many a contemporary truck. Bugatti's aim, however, was to produce a car which would surpass the best the world had to offer in every respect; before 1914 he had written of his dreams of building a super-car 'bigger than a Rolls-Royce and capable of cruising at 150 kph' (93 mph), but it was not until the 1920s that he could turn these dreams into reality.

Early in the spring of 1927, he invited a select group of journalists to his domain at Molsheim (Alsace) to see and ride in the prototype Golden Bug, the first, he claimed of a production run of twenty-five such chassis.

Riding on a wheelbase of 15 ft the prototype Type 41 Bugatti – the name Royale was not adopted until the early 1930s – was a car of superlatives.

W.F. Bradley, who was one of the first to ride in the car, noted: 'Although the car is very much bigger than any private vehicle yet built, it is so well proportioned that it does not give the impression of bulk. The bonnet is the longest ever seen, the track is wider and the wheelbase longer than on any existing car; the body tested on the prototype is a roomy seven-passenger open type taken from a high-class American car; the tyres have been made specially, and are a size usually associated with lorries; but there is no impression of being beside a monster'.

The most expensive motor car ever sold, the Type 41 Bugatti Royale Kellner coach, auctioned by Christie's in London's Albert Hall in 1987 for over £5 million. Yet the car had remained in the Bugatti family until after World War II, when it was acquired, along with a second Royale, by American sportsman Briggs Cunningham in a deal whose principal component was a brace of American refrigerators . . .

The Royale was in fact just an enlargement of normal Bugatti practice. It had the marque's typical forged hollow-section front axle with semi-elliptic springs passing through the beam, plus quarter-elliptic springs at the back, although, as a concession to the car's weight – some 3 tonnes – there were two sets of springs, the normal reversed 'coster-barrow' quarter-elliptics behind the axle, plus extra normal quarter-elliptics ahead of it.

The 14.7-litre straight-eight engine – the biggest road-going unit of the 1920s – was a gigantic version of the typical square-cut Bugatti power unit, with a single overhead camshaft operating three valves per cylinder. An ingenious point was the water-jacketing, which not only surrounded the cylinder bores, but which also extended downwards to cool the nine main bearings; three large tubular cross-members passing through the cylinder block supported the engine with exceptional rigidity. There was no flywheel, just a multi-plate clutch in a separate casing beneath the front seats, while the three-speed gearbox (ultra-low bottom for emergency hill-starts, direct drive for normal running and overdrive third) was built in unit with the rear axle.

Having taken ten years to bring his dream to reality, Ettore Bugatti was equally tardy in putting it into production, but he used the prototype as personal transportation, even venturing across the Alps with it in 1927 to open an Italian branch factory in Turin. The tourer bodywork – apparently adopted from that of a four-year-old Packard First Series Eight – was replaced in the following year by a curious coupé body designed like a nineteenth-century horsedrawn carriage, but this in turn was quickly supplanted by *Berline* coachwork. Still not satisfied, Bugatti replaced this body with yet another, this time a close-coupled 'coach' constructed by aviator-engineer C.T. Weymann, which won several *concours d'élégance* and was then written off in an accident when Ettore dozed off at the wheel. . . .

The first production Bugatti Type 41 did not appear until 1931; the power unit had been further developed and had a shorter stroke than did the prototype, reducing the swept volume to a mere 12 763 cc. It was, nevertheless, still the largest engine fitted to a production car in the post-Great War era.

It was at approximately this time that

RIGHT Typically Bugatti in its severity of line, the 12.7-litre engine of the Royale was the biggest road-going power unit of the 1920s and '30s. Although the Royale never enjoyed even the limited success envisioned by Ettore Bugatti, its power unit was later adapted for use in high-speed railcars.

the Royale name began to be applied to the Type 41, when Bugatti claimed in a sales catalogue that King Alfonso XIII of Spain had ordered a Royale: it wasn't true, although Alfonso was claimed to be awaiting delivery when in exile in France in 1932. Nor did the other kings – Boris of Bulgaria, Alexander of Yugoslavia and Carol of Romania – whose names were linked with the Royale actually place orders.

Parts were said to have been made for a production run of twenty-five cars, but, only three firm orders were ever received and of only six Royales actually built after the construction of the prototype, Ettore Bugatti retained three as family transportation. The first of these, the Coupé Napoleon, had elegant coupé de ville coachwork designed by Ettore's son Jean, still only in his early twenties.

It was followed by the Double Berline de Voyage, designed by Ettore on the lines of a nineteenth-century horsedrawn Diligence; with its stablemates, the Berline remained in the possession of the Bugatti family until 1951, when two of the three were sold. It belonged to a succession of well known American enthusiasts before entering the now-dispersed Harrah Collection, which then numbered well over one thousand cars.

When the bulk of Bill Harrah's cars were sold off after his death, the Berline de Voyage was sold for over $6 million, but this record was rapidly shattered when the car changed hands again in 1986 and was bought by pizza magnate Thomas Monaghan for $8.1 million (then equivalent to just under £5 million – and Monaghan had previously bought a brace of Duesenberg Model Js for over $1 million each).

The first Royale actually to be sold was delivered in 1932 to a French textile manufacturer named Armand Esders and fitted with two-seater roadster bodywork designed by Jean Bugatti. Remarkably, M Esders decided that he would never drive his new acquisition at night, and it therefore had no lamps. . . . This car was later sold to a French politician, who had it rebodied by Binder with coupé de ville coachwork – which failed to match up to the elegance of the original. This was carefully conserved by Binder, but was destroyed during a wartime air-raid on the nearby Citroën factory (André Citroën was another said, erroneously, to have ordered a Royale).

The first export sale of a Royale also came in 1932, when a chassis was shipped to Germany to be fitted with a coupé body by Weinberger of Munich to the order of a local surgeon, Dr Fuchs, who took the car both to Shanghai and to the United States, where he left it. It was later acquired by a General Motors vice-president named Charles Chayne, who modified the engine in some respects – among them, fitting quadruple down-draught carburettors in place of the twin side-draught units originally specified. Chayne eventually presented his Royale to the Henry Ford Museum in Dearborn, Michigan, where it is still displayed.

Already the Royale was entering the realms of automotive mythology. When in the summer of 1933 the third example of this model to be sold to a private

LEFT Even the wheels of the Royale were enormous, specially cast from aluminium and endowed with no fewer than thirty-two bolts to retain the detachable rims. Today, the only tyres suitable for this monster among motor cars are made for military vehicles

BOTH PAGES The extravagant nature of the Royale is underlined by its fanciful radiator mascot (right) in the shape of a dancing white elephant, derived from a work by Ettore's brother, the *animalier* sculptor, Rembrandt Bugatti. Despite this touch of whimsy, the proportions of the car are superb; it's difficult to realise that this vehicle has much the same wheelbase as a London bus. The sumptuous interior (below right) is of another Royale, the Coupé Napoleon, whose distinctive coachwork was one of the first designs of the young Jean Bugatti to come to fruition

customer was delivered to a British industrialist, Captain Cuthbert W. Fraser (who had its saloon bodywork constructed by Park Ward of Willesden, more usually associated with Rolls-Royce), *The Autocar* commented: 'The first Golden Bug to be built was constructed by the great Ettore Bugatti himself for his own personal use. This car was of golden hue and all the fittings were gold-plated (or were they solid gold?) . . . a favoured few were permitted to acquire a similar chassis, on the condition, it is believed, that they were taken to dinner at 'The Patron's' own house, and were officially approved'.

After Captain Fraser, however, there were no more orders. One more Royale was built, and given saloon bodywork by the great French coachbuilder Kellner. Again, it was used by the Bugatti family, and sold, in 1951, along with the *Berline de Voyage*, to that great American enthusiast Briggs Cunningham in a deal which involved relatively little money and two brand-new American refrigerators, which were unobtainable in France in the post-war years. Cunningham kept the car until 1987, when he sold the remainder of his collection to fellow enthusiast Miles Collier Jr; its London auction price of £5 million ($9 million) was an all-time record for any motor car.

Sought-after as they are in the 1980s, in their day the Bugatti Royales were truly white elephants, in recognition of which Ettore fitted several of the cars with an elephant radiator mascot derived from one of the celebrated *animalier* sculptures of his brother Rembrandt, who had committed suicide in 1916.

Having tooled up for the production of Royales on a larger scale than the out-of-joint times would permit, Ettore adapted the Type 41 engine to power (in sets of two or four) ultra-fast streamlined railcars capable of over 120 mph. These went into production in 1933; some eighty were built and the last remained in service until 1958.

So Bugatti Royale motoring was brought within the reach of every Frenchman who could afford the price of a railway ticket. . . .

BUGATTI TYPE 55

BOTH PAGES One of the most gorgeously proportioned two-seater bodies ever designed, the standard coachwork for the Bugatti Type 55 was created by Ettore Bugatti's young son, Jean; his mastery of the use of contrasting colours to emphasize the sweep line along the side of the bodywork was never better shown than in this beautiful car, which is today one of the stars of the Reims, France, motor museum owned by stylist Philippe Charbonneaux. His portfolio also includes the original concept for the Chevrolet Corvette

A Bugatti Type 55 roadster is today regarded as being among the most desirable of all sports cars and the few fortunate enough to own one are conscious that they are the possessors of one of the most aesthetically perfect two-seaters ever built. Yet only thirty years ago, the author watched a local garage owner saw up a Type 55 two-seater in order to create a hot rod. In the mid 1950s, not everyone appreciated the pure lines of Jean Bugatti's coachwork; this particular philistine was probably going to fit a streamlined glassfibre body of the type usually seen on time-expired Austin Seven and Ford Ten chassis in those days before compulsory vehicle testing, but the completed vehicle was never offered for inspection. It may well be that he eventually lost patience and abandoned the project.

For some time, the butchered remains of the body lay alongside the 'butcher's' workshop: the writer begged the horn,

In my biased opinion the Type 55 represents the most fascinating sports car ever built, and one capable of delighting the senses more than any other car, irrespective of price or year of manufacture.

A.C. Whincop, Bugatti expert, 1943

hoping it would add style to his Morgan three-wheeler, but its wiring was burnt out, so he eventually threw it away. That's the nearest he ever came to Bugatti ownership, but that broken Bugatti horn would probably now be worth more than the whole Type 55 was then!

The first Type 55 appeared in 1931 as a faster, more elegant, replacement for the Type 43 sports car. In many ways, it was a road-going Grand Prix car, its supercharged 2262 cc engine being virtually identical to that of the straight-eight Type 51 GP car, whose double-overhead-camshaft cylinder head was itself directly inspired by that of the front-wheel-drive American Miller racers which had been barnstormed round Europe in 1929 – and acquired by Ettore Bugatti for 'study'. The chassis was based on that of the Type 54 racing car, while the cast-aluminium wheels were of a pattern first seen on the Type 51.

It was the beautiful doorless roadster bodywork normally fitted to the Type 55 which made its fame, however, for the purity of line, the easy fluidity of the wings, represented a high point in automotive styling. It was the work of Bugatti's son Jean, then just twenty-one years old. Bugatti authority Paul Kestler calls the Type 55 *'un roadster à deux places d'une race stupéfiante'*, a phrase which needs no translation. The chassis was fully worthy of the body, too, for in 1932 Jean Bugatti drove a Type 55 from the Bugatti works at Molsheim, in Alsace, to Paris, a distance of some 280 miles, in 3 hr 47 min, an average speed of no less than 74 mph!

The Type 55 was first seen in Britain in the summer of 1932, when 'a neat black and red two-seater' appeared at the Bugatti Owners' Club speed trials on Race Hill, Lewes, and 'howled up the course with much smoke and dust in its wake' to win its class. The motoring press was bowled over by the virtues of the Type 55: in 1932 *Motor* praised it as 'a really comfortable, well sprung car with

ABOVE & RIGHT The casing projecting beneath the radiator of the Bugatti Type 55 houses not a supercharger but a dynastart, a combined dynamo/starter beloved of French sports-car makers of the era which was not entirely successful at either of its dual functions. Bugatti always claimed that he made his cars to go, not to stop, but this Type 55 at least carries a brake light (*right*)

superlative road-holding characteristics and a performance which is altogether exceptional ... the new Type 55 Bugatti is an ideal car for travelling safely from point to point at really high speeds and in complete comfort.'

In 1937 H.S. Linfield of *The Autocar* tested the actual 1933 Motor Show car, which by then had over 14 000 miles on the clock, and was offered at £595 against its new price of £1350 (in 1932 that made it the most expensive two-seater sports car on the British market). Despite the 55's age, Linfield was mightily impressed: 'On the road this Bugatti was a veritable joy', he said. 'This feeling was not only due entirely to the performance available, but also to the superlative manner in which the car steered and cornered.... Apart from some remarkable figures on the indirect gears, the flexibility of the engine on its quite high top gear (4.15:1) was an outstanding feature.'

Indeed, in the hands of its original owner, Embiricos, that particular Type 55 had been used for both Continental touring and racing, and had covered a half-mile at Brooklands in racing trim at 124 mph, running on methanol. On road fuel – a cocktail of Cleveland Discol pump petrol and neat benzole – the maximum was around 112 mph, and the average fuel consumption was in the region of 11.5 mpg.

'So excellent were the stability and general handling,' wrote Linfield, 'that the car was "wished" round corners, rock-steady and feeling completely safe, yet the suspension was really comfortable for a machine of this type.' Years later, Allen Jones, who ran the Wiltshire tea rooms which the *Autocar* testers used as a turning point, claimed that the main purpose of Linfield's test run had been to gather holly for his Christmas decorations, it being a few days before Christmas 1936. 'There was certainly a pair of secateurs in the car to prove the statement, but the charms of high-speed motoring proved too strong and there

was not a berry on board in spite of 200 miles that afternoon!' Added Jones: 'My first impression was that it was the coldest car I had ever been in; the body was a very French grand sport type, with no doors and practically no sides either, and it was freezing hard that evening ... it took us half an hour to get the engine warm enough to start the journey home, piling the bonnet with rugs and running at about 1500 rpm; once ready, it returned to Esher in 1 hour 45 minutes, although I still wonder how the crew survived the cold.'

The Type 55 Bugatti roadster has become such a classic design that it is difficult to realise on how few cars that reputation has been built: between 1932 and 1935, the Molsheim factory built just thirty-eight examples of this model, and fewer than half survive today. If he's still alive, that sacreligious garage owner of yore will surely be kicking himself for his personal contribution to that attenuated survival rate....

ABOVE The flat-spoked, cast-aluminium wheels of the Type 55 recall Bugatti's first aluminium wheels, fitted to the Type 35 Grand Prix car of 1924. Nowadays regarded as the ultimate in sporting chic, the original rationale of aluminium wheels was that they were cheaper to make than wire wheels

OVERLEAF The Bugatti Type 55 wasn't only beautiful, it was also a remarkably effective sports car: in 1932, Jean Bugatti drove a Type 55 from Molsheim to Paris at an average speed of 74 mph

BUGATTI TYPE 57

The Bugatti Type 57 was Jean Bugatti's masterpiece, and it was endowed with some of the finest coachwork of its day – and some of the most bizarre. Striking the happy medium between extravagance and good taste is this 1939 drophead coupé by Saoutchik

T he Type 57, the finest road-going Bugatti of them all, first appeared at the 1933 Paris Salon as a replacement for the Type 49, but the 2.8-litre engine capacity was really the only thing the two Bugattis had in common.

Technically, the twin-cam Type 57 was remarkable evidence of the rapid rise to maturity of Ettore Bugatti's son Jean, who was only 21 when the car first appeared. He and Bartolomeo ('Meo') Costatini, Bugatti's racing manager, collaborated on the chassis design, with Costatini proposing independent front suspension for the new model and Jean wanting left-hand steering.

The imperious Ettore overruled them both, though he did permit a curious

design of split front axle, whose two halves were united by a screwed-on collar so that slight movement could occur to eliminate torque reaction under braking. It was a total failure; cars built with this curious axle were quickly returned to the Bugatti works to have the collar brazed solid. Ettore also insisted that the twin-cam cylinder head be fixed.

The Type 57C Bugatti is incontestably one of the fastest grand touring cars there is. . . . The average speed attainable with the Type 57C Bugatti is not dependent upon the car, but is merely limited by road conditions.
Charles Faroux, *La Vie Automobile*

The Type 57 was, however, the first Bugatti car to have its transmission in unit with the engine. Originally intended to be 2866 cc, the swept volume of this engine was increased to 3257 cc, the same as that of the superseded single-cam Type 49. With a five-bearing crankshaft, the straight-eight engine had its cylinder block cast in unit with the head, whose hemispherical combustion chambers were fully machined to make good use of the twin-cam layout. The potential of the new car was effectively demonstrated when it was shown to British enthusiasts for the first time, at the Bugatti Owners' Club sprint at Lewes, Sussex, on 21 October 1933, by Jean Bugatti, who was guest of honour. His Type 57 saloon was faster over the course than the official winner of the over-1500 cc touring class. . . .

Not only did Jean Bugatti design the car and its 'catalogue' coachwork, but he was originally responsible for demonstrating it to dealers and prospective clients. Unfortunately, the kind of driving that enabled him to beat racing cars in a standard saloon was, it seems, too much for Ettore, who ordered the demonstration work to be taken over by works racing driver René Dreyfus, who, between Grands Prix, also delivered chassis from the factory to the carrossier Gangloff in nearby Colmar.

Standard bodywork for the Type 57 included the Atalante *faux-cabriolet*, the Ventoux 'coach' (a two-door saloon), the Stelvio coupé, the Galibier saloon, the Aravis convertible coupé (only built in 1939) and the spectacular Atlantic coupé (originally known as the 'Aerolithe'), whose fluid body lines were embellished by distinctive riveted spines down the centreline of body and wings. Among the leading coachbuilders which also bodied the Type 57 were James Young, Corsica

BELOW The rear aspect of this Type 57 is particularly agreeable; Saoutchik has subjugated his normal tendency to exaggerate the bright-metal sweeps along the wings and flanks of the car and reduced them to very effective contrast lines

LEFT & BELOW A sign of
changing times: Jean Bugatti
persuaded his father that the
Type 57 should be endowed
with hydraulic, rather than
mechanical, brakes to match
the performance offered by
the car, particularly in
supercharged form. Under the
bonnet, the master cylinder
gives the game away . . .

and Gurney Nutting in England, Van
Vooren, Franay, Letourner & Marchand,
Saoutchik, Guillore, Figoni & Falaschi and
Labourdette in France and Graber in
Switzerland.

In August 1936, Bugatti introduced the
Type 57S, a sports version of the Type
57, which returned to the split front axle
layout, this time, with torque rods to
prevent twist. It had a shorter wheelbase
than the normal Type 57, the rear axle
passing through large holes formed in the
very deep chassis side-members. Initially,
the 57S had the traditional Bugatti
horseshoe radiator, but soon a handsome
vee-radiator perfectly suited to Jean
Bugatti's lithe-lined coachwork was
standardized.

Perhaps Jean Bugatti's wildest creation
was the sports roadster shown at the
1936 Paris Salon on the Type 57S chassis,
with all-enveloping spats on the front
wheels, the spats being split and their
forward part swivelling as the steering
was turned. This extraordinary car was
bought by the painter André Derain.

A second series of Type 57s appeared
in late 1936, based on an improved
chassis. That year also saw the simple

Hartford friction dampers originally fitted
replaced by complex De Ram units, which
gave damping proportional to the speed
of the car, although these in turn were
replaced by Allinquant telescopic units.

More significant, perhaps, was that Jean
Bugatti persuaded his father that the Type
57 should have hydraulic, rather than
mechanical, brakes. Since Ettore had
always maintained 'I make my cars to go,
not to stop!' this was no mean victory.
Better braking had become essential from

the moment that, in October 1936, the first chassis had been produced with a factory-fitted supercharger. Known as the Type 57C (for *compresseur*), this new model had a top speed of 106 mph against the 93 mph of the normal Type 57 and also gained in flexibility.

The Type 57S was also soon available with a supercharger; known as Type 57SC, this was probably the finest Bugatti of all with a top speed of 135 mph. 'I would say', remarked Peter Hampton, one of Britain's most discriminating connoisseurs of thoroughbred motor cars, 'without doubt, it is the fastest sports car in the world. The road-holding and cornering of the 57S and SC have to be experienced to be believed.'

Of a total production of some 750 Type 57 Bugattis, only thirty or so were built as Type 57SCs, but many of the forty Type 57Ss produced were retrospectively fitted with superchargers.

In all its incarnations, the Type 57 Bugatti was an exceptional car, and proved this in 1936, when a racing Type 57 made its debut. Fitted with enveloping streamlined 'Tank' bodywork, the Type 57G Bugatti had a Type 57S engine in a Type 57 chassis. The 57G of Jean-Pierre Wimille and Raymond Sommer won the 1936 French sports car Grand Prix, then later that year Wimille, Veyron and Williams took the Class C·(3 – 5 litres) 24-hour record at the Montlhéry circuit, south of Paris, covering 2991 miles at an average speed of over 124 mph. This was no less than 20 mph faster than the existing record.

In 1937, Wimille again made motor racing history with a Type 57G Tank, this time winning the Le Mans 24-hour race, with Robert Benoist as co-driver, and setting a new lap record of 96.31 mph. This French victory was a great psychological boost to the nation, for it ended ten years of British and Italian domination of the French classic.

The Bugatti Tanks did not run during the crisis summer of 1938, but an improved version, based on a Type 57C chassis and engine, with Type 59 wheels and a higher-ratio rear axle, won the 1939 Le Mans at a new record speed of 86.6 mph, driven by Wimille and Veyron.

A few weeks later, Jean Bugatti was testing this car on a closed stretch of public highway near the Bugatti works at Molsheim, Alsace, when a drunken cyclist appeared from the verge and wobbled into the Tank's path. Jean swerved to avoid the man, crashed into the ditch, and was killed instantly. He was only twenty-seven but he was irreplaceable, and neither Ettore Bugatti nor his company recovered from the loss.

BOTH PAGES Even though the Bugatti Type 57 was a sports car without parallel, it could be endowed with remarkably civilized bodywork; that such a degree of luxury could be combined with such performance in 1939 is remarkable proof of the pace of progress – at least where hand-built sports cars were concerned!

CADILLAC V16

The Cadillac sixteen-cylinder engine goes far beyond the contemporary conception of brilliant performance. It multiplies power and subdivides it into a continuous flow . . . constantly at full-volume efficiency . . . flexible . . . instantly responsive. This, plus complete individuality in styling, is — in brief — the story of the 'V16'.

Cadillac advertisement, 1930

Imagine a car so refined that the only sound audible when the engine is ticking over is the tiny electric spark created as the ignition contacts separate, a car which breaks new ground in riding comfort, a car which its makers could justifiably describe as 'the very finest of its kind . . . a mechanical masterpiece'.

Then imagine the sensation that must have been caused when that car — the

V16 Cadillac – was launched in January 1930, for it was the very first sixteen-cylinder car to go into production, a defiant thumbing of the nose at the depression that was even then engulfing the United States and a proud assertion of Cadillac's supremacy among luxury cars.

The creation of the V16 Cadillac had been a reaction by its makers, General Motors, to the loss of their traditional first place in the luxury car class to Packard, who in the mid 1920s moved ahead of Cadillac by a ratio of more than two to one in terms of sales. Since Packard had pioneered series production of the V12 engine with their 1915 Twin Six, which had over-topped Cadillac's V8, Cadillac determined that their response to Packard's takeover of what they regarded as their rightful place should be faster,

The Depression was at its worst when the V16 Cadillac was launched, yet to look at this 1931 phaeton it would be impossible to realise that grim fact. However, in that year, most of the 750 V16 Cadillacs sold were left over from the previous year, despite generous dealer discounts

RIGHT Not only does the V16 Cadillac phaeton boast a second speedometer so that the rear-seat passenger can keep an eye on what his chauffeur is up to, it also has a retractable rear windscreen, controlled by the handle below the secondary instrument panel. The elegant body is by Fleetwood, in-house *carrossier* to General Motors

OVERLEAF The V16 Cadillac Fleetwood phaeton features Pilot-Ray lamps which, thanks to linking rods, turn with the steering

more powerful and refined than anything else on the market.

Militating against the use of a V12 power unit was the fact that Packard had been first in that field, so that Cadillac could be accused of plagiarism and suffer by comparison. So a sixteen-cylinder powerplant was developed in remarkable secrecy by Cadillac's new engine designer, Owen Nacker, while the entire project was masterminded by the company's Chief Engineer, Ernest Seaholm. Most of the junior engineers and outside suppliers involved in the new model programme were convinced that Cadillac was developing a new commercial vehicle, for the blueprints were mostly marked 'Bus' or 'Coach', and since the body styling and prototype work was also performed in-house by General Motors' Fleetwood division, the launch of the V16 Cadillac took the press and industry by surprise. The legendary silence of the Cadillac's power unit was achieved by its hydraulic tappet dampers – the first time that this principle had been put into series pro-duction – which brought unprecedented refinement to the car's running.

Sales of the new car got off to a good start, despite the depression. By April 1930, the one-thousandth V16 was being shipped and in June the two-thousandth left the factory, while sales income reached the $13.5 million mark. The first six months of V16 Cadillac production, however, represented fifty-two per cent of output during the model's seven-year life – and nearly 46 per cent of Cadillac's total output of V16 cars. Only 500 V16s were sold in the latter half of 1930, while in the heavily depressed market of 1931 sales – mostly of cars left over from the previous year – totalled just 750, despite keen discounting by Cadillac dealers. In 1933, Cadillac announced that it would build only 400 V16s, but actually made a mere 126 and from then on V16 production averaged fifty cars a year until the model dropped out of the production schedules during 1937.

The fate of the V16 had been sealed when Cadillac announced in August 1930 that they were to build a V12, using the biggest of their V8 chassis and costing from $1555 to $4305 less than the comparable V16 models, which retailed at prices from $5350 to $9200. From the outset, the V12 outsold the V16 to such an extent that when both models were withdrawn in 1937 Cadillac were selling ten V12s to every one of the V16s.

Sales success was perhaps not the prime purpose of the Cadillac V16 however: its aim was to re-establish Cadillac as the pace-setter of the luxury car market and in that it succeeded brilliantly. Indeed, even Rolls-Royce were not too proud to learn from the Cadillac V16 when they developed their V12 Phantom III, which had hydraulic valve silencers and Cadillac-style coil-and-wishbone independent front suspension (designed by Maurice Olley – who had joined General Motors from the depression-hit American Rolls-Royce factory – and adopted for 1934).

The bespoke nature of the Cadillac V16 was evident from the variety of coachwork catalogued for this costly chassis: up to twenty individual body styles were available in a single year, many of them only built in 'production runs' of one or two cars. Of the early examples, the most famous was the 1930 'Madame X' series, whose curious name was chosen after General Motors' chief of styling, Harley Earl, had seen a 'time-tested tear-jerker' talking picture at the Fisher Theater in Detroit. The orotund Earl thought that the character of Madame X – 'different, mysterious, exciting and, above all ... intriguing' – reflected the design objectives of a no-expense-spared V16 model that was then being developed in the GM Art and Color Studios – and thus the new car was named Madame X.

Distinguished by a raked windscreen with thin pillars, Madame X Cadillacs had such costly embellishments as stainless-steel coach striping instead of painted lines, gold-faced instruments and stainless-steel wire wheels. Naturally, when Hollywood made a new version of the film, a Madame X Cadillac co-starred....

In 1937, the V16 Cadillac was replaced – by a new V16! Although the new car was still a luxury model, the old extravagances were set aside and the

design was simplified – the new power unit, its cylinders set at such a wide angle that it was virtually a flat-sixteen, had side, instead of overhead, valves – to reflect the changed conditions of the late 1930s. Only 508 examples of the 1938 car were sold in its two-year production life, for the V8 Cadillacs of the period were so smooth, flexible and powerful that the vastly more expensive V16 was redundant.

Better to remember the original Cadillac V16, of which no less a judge than W.O. Bentley said: 'My chief memories of this automobile (although that term is inadequate) were its astonishing refinement with perhaps the most completely successful elimination of evidence that explosions were occurring under the bonnet ever obtained in a motor car.

'The word "torque" also took on a new meaning with this V16, which could reach 90 mph with a sort of endless limousine body of goodness knows what weight'.

Small wonder that Cadillac could proudly boast in their advertising of their cars setting 'The Standard of the World'.

ABOVE & OVERLEAF
Extravagance made metal: this massive 1930 Cadillac V16 is only a two-seater, one of the very first bodies to be built by the famous Italian *carrozziere* Pinin Farina, who had just broken away from the family firm of Stabilimenti Farina to establish his own business

L̲ouis Delage, history concludes, was not a nice chap to know: in his prosperous days, this one-eyed engineer from Cognac (where he was born in 1874), scandalised polite society with his public womanising, his string of dancers and actresses. Nor was he a nice man to work with: when during World War II the Delage factory was accused of criminal negligence in the manufacture of munitions for the French Army, Louis Delage let his production manager, Maurice Gaultier, take the blame – and the five-year prison sentence; again, when he could have made the name of an unknown young engineer, Nemorin Causan, a household word – Causan had designed the 1257 cc single-cylinder engine, with four valves and two sparking plugs, for the Delage racer which won the 1908 Coupe des Voiturettes – Louis Delage set principle aside by taking a bribe from engine manufacturers De Dion-Bouton to say that the winning car was De Dion powered.

This glorious Delage D8S Grand Sport Roadster with Letourneur & Marchand coachwork was road-tested in 1931 by *The Autocar*, who concluded: 'Clearly, this new Delage is one of the exceptional machines of the day'. And certainly there was something out of the ordinary about the 100 mph performance of the super sports Delage, for very few cars of the day were capable of lapping the Brooklands track at such a speed in touring trim

At Olympia this year there are many fine cars . . . new miracles of mechanical genius . . . new beauty in bodywork . . . new luxury . . . splendid cars, brilliant cars, great cars. . . . But the greatest of them all is the Delage Straight Eight – the most talked of car in the motoring world today. Search at the Show for the car built solely for performance – its capabilities will not exceed those of the Delage Straight Eight. Study all the coachwork at the Show – you will find none so sumptuous in line and luxury as the great variety of individual bodies now available for every type of Delage chassis. . . . Compare the Delage and every car at Olympia at over double the price – does any car in the whole world give you so much for so little?
Delage advertisement, 1930

When it came to making the finest cars on the roads of France, however, Louis Delage was single-mindedly devoted to a creed of perfection: 'Make only one thing – but make it well'. Delage had struck out on his own in 1905, after learning his craft with an obscure company named Turgan-Foy (whose cars had *vertical* crankshafts) and the oldest French car maker, Peugeot. Starting with a meagre borrowed capital of 35 000 francs (£1400), Delage brought out his first complete car in December 1905, a voiturette with a single-cylinder De Dion engine. By the end of 1908, annual sales had risen to over three hundred cars, and by 1912 the three hundred workmen were turning out a range of four- and six-cylinder cars in a big new factory; the company was also successfully racing fast and powerful cars of advanced design.

Delage dramatically changed their image after the war, producing large luxury cars rather than the small and medium-sized models with which they had established their reputation. The first of these much-admired Delages was the CO of 1918; powered by a 4532 cc six-cylinder engine, it was developed into the CO2 in 1921, but never achieved the popularity that Louis Delage had anticipated – fewer than 1600 of both types were built instead of the three thousand a year that Delage had forecast,

BOTH PAGES Today, the Letourneur & Marchand Grand Sport Roadster belongs to Delage collector André Surmain: in 1931, it was the star of the Delage stand at the Olympia Motor Show, although in those days it wore its headlamps at the front of its pontoon wings. Used as a rally car, it crashed ... At the heart of the D8 Delage (*above*) is the magnificent Gaultier-designed, straight-eight, 4-litre engine, which in D8S form developed 120 bhp. But, thanks to the Depression, only ninety-nine D8S Delages found purchasers

and the company's fortunes had to be re-established with the less-exotic 2120 cc DI model, of which 9284 were made in five years. This was the basis for the finest sporting Delages of the decade, the DIS and the low-chassis DISS; just 983 of these long-legged sports cars were built.

If the marque was prospering, Louis Delage's relationships with his designers were no happier than before, and after he had fired his engineer-cousin Planchon, and Planchon's assistant Escure had resigned to grow grapes, Delage brought back Gaultier, at liberty and working for the Georges Irat company, as Chief Engineer. After starting with a dismal but inexplicably successful side-valve six, the DR, Gaultier produced his masterpiece at the Paris Salon in October 1929. The 4061 cc Delage D8 had a straight-eight

overhead-valve power unit developing 105 bhp and was built to the most exacting standards; it was a car which was worthy of being placed alongside the Hispano-Suiza, but which sold for about one-third of that car's price – £685 against £1950 in chassis form.

Even Gabriel Voisin, not one to worry about finance, said that he didn't know how Delage could afford to sell such fine cars at such low prices – and the inevitable bankruptcy proved that Louis Delage didn't know either.... When the house of cards began to crumble in 1933, a rescue bid was blocked by Delage's wife, doubtless weary of her husband's succession of mistresses and wanting to stem the flow of funds that allowed her husband his dalliances; however, before the final crash came in 1935, Delage

FAR LEFT The Marchal headlamps of the D8S are nowadays more conventionally mounted, but the frontal aspect of the car, with its thermostatically operated radiator shutters, is still impressive. Below the headlamps is a pair of ingeniously designed foglamps

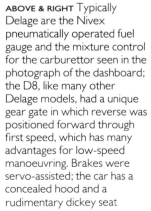

ABOVE & RIGHT Typically Delage are the Nivex pneumatically operated fuel gauge and the mixture control for the carburettor seen in the photograph of the dashboard; the D8, like many other Delage models, had a unique gear gate in which reverse was positioned forward through first speed, which has many advantages for low-speed manoeuvring. Brakes were servo-assisted; the car has a concealed hood and a rudimentary dickey seat

managed to produce over 1900 D8 chassis. The marque lived on until 1953 as an *alter ego* of Delahaye.

In its heyday, the D8 Delage, bodied by France's finest *carrossiers*, was the chosen transport of French high society: black singer Josephine Baker, the toast of *tout Paris*, had an elegant drophead bodied by Letourneur & Marchand.

Finest of all the D8 variants was the rare D8S super sports version, described as 'the best road car Delage ever built', and one of the rarest – just ninety-nine were built. With a tuned engine developing 120 bhp, the D8S was one of the few cars of its day genuinely capable

of achieving 100 mph on the road, a phenomenal performance for a 4-litre pushrod engine.

Testing a two-seated D8S in 1931, *The Autocar* waxed lyrical: 'Even today, when 100 mph has become commonplace for racing cars, there is something almost faintly fantastical about such a speed for a comfortable, touring-type car which can be used just as effectively for general purposes, including town work ... clearly, this new Delage is one of the exceptional machines of the day.'

The fortunate few who own D8S Delages today must surely echo those words of praise.

Dating from the end of Delage D8 production is this 1939 Figoni & Falaschi-bodied D8120 tourer with its flamboyant wing treatment and external exhausts. But instead of the Gaultier engine, this last of the Delage straight-eights is fitted with a Delahaye power unit

DELAHAYE TYPE 135

Until 1935, the existence of the Delahaye company was stolid and unexciting, its products mostly sound, reliable touring cars, lorries and fire-engines. One of its few eccentricities was the first production car with a V6 power unit, the not entirely successful 2565 cc Type 44 of 1914. Then, in 1935, Delahaye kicked over the traces and brought out one of the most outstanding French sports cars of the period, a car which was capable of winning such strenuous events as the Monte Carlo Rally, the Coupe des Alpes, Le Mans and the Pau Grand Prix.

It was as though a respectable bank clerk, after four decades of a blameless career, had overnight become a rakish national sporting hero, swapping his staid pinstripes for a suit in the latest cut and colours. Yet at heart the sensational new Delahaye 135 was still a stolid bourgeois, for its 3.5-litre engine was directly derived from a power unit developed for one of

There are few cars with such superb road-holding and steering, such performance, and such instantly responsive controls.
The Motor, 1938

the company's lorries – but it was still among the most classic power units of the 1930s. That robust engine was installed in a strong, boxed chassis and the car was endowed with outstanding handling characteristics by transverse-spring independent front suspension, which, averred a contemporary road-tester, 'took all the sting out of any bad surface'.

It would be easy to think that the Delahaye 135 was a direct result of the acquisition of the financially troubled Delage company by Delahaye in 1935, but that wasn't the case at all; indeed, from 1936 on, Delages became effectively Delahayes in all but name, and the roots of Delahaye's new lease of life can be found in the appointment of

Jean-François as chief engineer by 'Monsieur Charles' Weiffenbach, who had owned the company since 1906.

Jean-François had created one of the more intriguing light cars of the 1920s, the all-independently sprung overhead-camshaft 1.5-litre Beck, which caused a sensation at the 1920 Brussels Salon and then vanished from the scene two years later. The first sign that a wind of change

was blowing through the stuffy corridors of the Delahaye headquarters under his aegis came with the introduction of the 3.25-litre Type 138 Superlux at the 1933 Paris Salon.

A short-wheelbase 18CV Sport version of this was developed for the following year, triple carburettors boosting its power output from 90 to 100 bhp; a team of these cars won their class in the Coupe des Alpes, and it was from this model that the Type 135 was developed, using a lowered chassis and the choice of a competition 'crash' gearbox, a synchromesh transmission for touring or a Wilson preselector unit.

The success of the equation was shown when Delahaye 135s bored out to 3.5 litres and specially developed to meet the regulations of the French Sports Car

During World War II, Delahaye became part of the Groupe Française Automobile, organized by Baron Petiet to keep production going under the German Occupation of France. Although the GFA was disbanded in 1952, all post-war Delahayes – like this 1947 135M – bore its initials on their radiators

BOTH PAGES The 1947 Delahaye 135M (*right*) wears drophead coupé coachwork by the Belgian *carrossier* Van den Plas. The British importers of the Delahaye, Selbourne (Mayfair) Limited were fulsome in their praise of the post-war model: 'The Delahaye 135M is a superlative machine built with great care and precision based on the fruits of long experience. It is designed to give its owner many thousands of miles of fast, trouble-free motoring under any conditions of road and weather'

Grand Prix formula finished 2–3–4–5 in the 1936 French Sports Car Grand Prix and won the 1937 and 1939 Monte Carlo Rallies, the 1938 Le Mans race and the 'Fastest Sports Car' challenge race at Brooklands in 1939, against a 2.9-litre Alfa Romeo and a 4-litre Darracq.

For road use, the 135 was available with either the 3.25-litre engine or a 3.5-litre unit. The smaller engine was normally installed in the Coupe des Alpes model, and it was one of these that a wartime road-tester found 'could go round corners without any effort at all at a general sort of rate around 50 to 60, and took the hills without much slackening, and with very little more throttle – an outstanding machine for acceleration and cornering; there is no "give" at all in a fast bend'. Even on wartime low-octane Pool petrol, the engine gave around 18 mpg without excessive pinking, while high overall gearing enabled the car to travel along 'in an extraordinarily easy way'; steering and gearchange were exceptionally quick and light in action.

From 1937, the Delahaye 135 could also be specified with a Cotal electrically

ABOVE & RIGHT The engine of the Delahaye 135 (*above*) was derived from a six-cylinder truck engine – but it was one of the classic sporting power units of the 1930s. In triple-carburettor form it developed some 130 bhp and could propel a heavily bodied Delahaye at a genuine 100 mph. The 1938 Delahaye 135MS (*right*) has sports-roadster bodywork

controlled epicyclic transmission, which gave exceptionally fast up-and-down gear-changing without the use of the clutch, the metal-in-oil plate clutches controlling the gear trains within the 'box being actuated by solenoids when a miniature gear lever beneath the steering wheel selected the appropriate ratio. A peculiarity of the Cotal transmission was that all four ratios could be used in reverse, and racing driver Rob Walker managed to invert his 135 in spectacular fashion while trying top-ratio reverse (on a car capable of 105 mph in a forward direction!).

The 135 was bodied by such famous *carrossiers* as Figoni & Falaschi (irreverently nicknamed 'Phoney and Flashy' by the British), Chapron and Letourneur & Marchand; perhaps the finest of all the Type 135s were those with Figoni & Falaschi roadster bodies, with wondrously opulent curves and

ballooning wings which epitomised luxury in every line. It's quite remarkable that, alongside such bespoke elegance, Delahaye continued to build lorries and armoured vehicles.

After the war, the 135 was revived and in 1947, the standard factory bodywork was styled by Phillipe Charbonneux. The following year saw Delahaye launching the 4.5-litre 175; then, in 1951, came the last new Delahayes, a Delahaye-built Jeep and the 3.5-litre 235. Delage faded from the scene in 1952 and Delahaye car production was purely nominal when Hotchkiss acquired the company in 1954. For a few months after the takeover, lorries, known as 'Hotchkiss-Delahaye', were built, but after a brief interval, they were simply called 'Hotchkiss'.

The Delahaye marque had survived exactly sixty years; it was quite remarkable that its last two decades were also its greatest.

The elegant peak of 1930s styling – a 1938 Delahaye 135MS sports-roadster. A total of some 3000 Type 135 Delahayes is believed to have been built, but only the select few had such outstanding coachwork. Rarest of all were the competition two-seaters … but a thriving trade in the construction of replicas of Delahaye sports racers has developed in recent years

DELAHAYE TYPE 145

In 1935, Delahaye designer Jean-François created a spectacular Type 145, a 4.5-litre V12 derivative of the Type 135. Three camshafts in the crankcase controlled its overhead valves and three dual-choke Stromberg carburettors earned the power unit the nickname of 'the gasworks'. Rear suspension was by a de Dion axle.

Claimed Delahaye advertising for the Type 145: 'It's the incomparable competition car which gives its drivers all the joys of the struggle crowned with the immense satisfaction of speed and victory. . . .'

The truth of this assertion was demonstrated in 1937, when the Automobile Club de France, seeking to regain French national prestige, offered a purse of a million francs to the constructor who, before 31 August, could beat the record speed of 146.508 kph set by Mercedes in 1935, over a distance of 200 km.

Just four days short of the deadline, driving a 250 bhp racing Type 145, René Dreyfus managed to break the Mercedes record by a narrow margin (he averaged 146.654 kph over 200 km at Montlhéry) to win the prize. Of the other two potential challengers, Bugatti broke a piston and the untried SEFAC failed to make the attempt. It is said, however, that with Gallic guile, the ACF managed to split the prize between the *unsuccessful* candidates!

The Type 145 made a brave attempt on that impregnably Italian event, the Mille Miglia, in April 1938. The car, driven by René Dreyfus, with Varet as co-driver, had been fitted with two-seater sports coachwork, which the French thought '*un peu esthetique*'. *The Autocar* was even more forthright. 'So this is a sports car!' ran the caption to a photograph of

It is the car that is missing from the French market . . . its performance is limitless. It doesn't depend on the mechanism, nor on the driver. It only depends on the road conditions. . . .

Delahaye advertisement for the Type 145

Dreyfus's car. 'The twelve-cylinder Delahaye in Mille Miglia form certainly looks extraordinary.'

Even though one of the cars had been timed at 165 mph on the Reims Grand Prix circuit, as a sports-racer the Type 145 was already passé; so in 1938 Delahaye transformed the twelve-cylinder car into a luxury road-going machine and designated it Type 165. The three-carburettor installation was replaced by a solitary dual-choke Solex, the magneto ignition by twin coils and the de Dion rear suspension by a conventional live axle.

Nevertheless, even in this detuned form – power output was claimed to be 160 bhp – the Type 165 was still capable of 115 mph. It was launched at the 1938 Paris Salon, a show postponed by a fortnight because of the political situation, and the show car, an amazing red Figoni & Falaschi roadster with fully faired front wheels, caused a sensation.

'A very speedy effect is obtained' noted *The Autocar*, 'by continuing the shallow louvres on the bonnet in the form of two bands of chromium tapering to a point near the tail, the door handle being recessed in this band of metal. These two bands, going from radiator to tail, are the only relief to the uniform red of the body.'

The Type 165 wasn't seen at the 1938 London Motor Show, which clashed with the postponed Paris Salon, but it was offered on the British market at £1480, which made it cheaper than the V12 Lagonda of identical engine capacity. The Figoni two-seater was acquired by holiday camp magnate Billy Butlin, but it's uncertain whether the Type 165 ever passed the prototype stage.

At the 1939 New York Show, a Delahaye V12 with Figoni bodywork was shown; it was a drophead with disappearing hood and patented retractable windscreen. After the war a Type 145 was converted into a cabriolet by Franay for Prince Rainier of Monaco. There was a legacy of 145 in the post-war Type 175 six-cylinder model, in that this 1946 car had the hydraulic brakes and Dubonnet independent front suspension of the touring 165 and the de Dion rear axle of the 145 racer. The Figoni & Falaschi bodywork of the Type 175 shown at Olympia in 1950 was as opulent as ever, although it had Figoni's curious 'narwhal' protruberance above the radiator shell. Swooping chrome bands delineated the spatted wings, and *The Autocar* said that its 'extraordinary blending of bumper and grille shapes make this 4.5-litre Delahaye a magnet at the Show'.

The Type 175 lasted only until 1951, with around 150 being built. Delahaye was a dying company by then; the post-war French political and fiscal climate was not one for a large luxury car to flourish in and only seventy examples of the company's last car, the Type 235 of 1951–3, left the factory. It was the end of a remarkable era.

ABOVE & LEFT Rather like an ill-favoured lady recalled in Gabriel Voisin's scurrilous memoirs, the Delahaye 145 racer's bodywork is 'temptation at the rear, compassion at the front'; its triple-carburetted V12 engine (*left*), nicknamed 'the gasworks', developed some 250 bhp

OVERLEAF The twelve-cylinder Type 145 was the basis for the road-going Type 165 Delahaye; this Type 145 is one of the exhibits in the Charbonneaux museum at Reims

DUESENBERG MODEL J

This Figoni-styled Duesenberg Model J 'French Speedster' was commissioned from Parisian coachbuilder Fernandez by the company's French importer Edmund Z. Sadovich for the Paris-Nice Rally and the Cannes Concours d'Elégance in 1931. Sadovich sold fourteen Duesenbergs from his stand at the 1931 Paris Salon, presenting the car as 'the fastest, most beautiful, most powerful and most expensive car in the world'

Just as the Rolls-Royce name came to be synonymous with the peak of excellence, so the name of America's finest car quickly entered that nation's folklore. Even now, fifty years after the Duesenberg went out of production, Americans who have never seen a Model J will describe anything truly outstanding as 'a real Duesy'. The magic of the Duesenberg name is still potent: it's some years since American pizza magnate Thomas Monaghan paid over a million dollars each for his two Duesenbergs, and

the marque that was once decried by dyed-in-the-wool British enthusiasts as 'uncompromisingly brash' has become one of the world's most desirable motor cars.

In its heyday, the Duesenberg's credentials were impeccable: its creators, Fred S. Duesenberg and his brother August had been working in the motor industry since the turn of the century and had made their name as manufacturers of high-performance engines. In 1920, the first passenger car to bear the

Duesenberg name had also been America's first production car with a straight-eight engine, aluminium pistons and four-wheel hydraulic brakes. In the following year, a Duesenberg straight-eight racer – the first Grand Prix car to be fitted with hydraulic four-wheel brakes – brought America victory in the French Grand Prix. Five years later, however, Fred Duesenberg's uncompromising passion for engineering perfection outdistanced his abilities as a financier and brought his company to its knees.

'The superlatively fine has no need to be boastful. Always there is devotion to an ideal with only one thought in mind: to produce the best, forgetful of cost or expediency or any other consideration. When this is finally accomplished, the work is acclaimed a masterpiece by those who are in a position to know; it is recognised as a standard by which all other things of its kind are judged . . . this is true whether the creation be a Taj Mahal, a Grecian vase, Cellini's metal craft, a Rembrandt painting – or a Duesenberg car.'
Duesenberg Model J catalogue

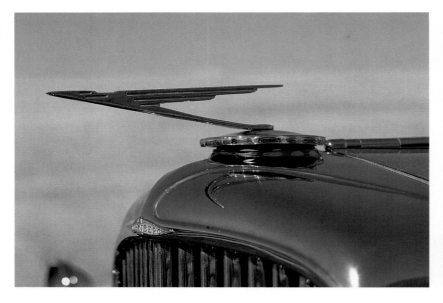

ABOVE & RIGHT Styled by Gordon Buehrig, the 'Duesenbird' mascot (*above*) first appeared in 1931; it cost $25 as an optional extra, but was fitted to the majority of Duesenbergs – almost 300 of them, including the French Speedster. But unlike the majority of Duesenbergs, the Speedster – now in the Blackhawk Collection in California – has analogue 'sweep-needle' speedometer and tachometer faces (*below right*); usually, American-style drum instruments were fitted. Another odd feature is that the tachometer reads *anti-clockwise....* This 1931 car, built as a Model J, has been fitted with a supercharger in recent years to bring it up to SJ standard and the original louvred bonnet replaced by one tailored to external exhaust pipes (*above right*)

Salvation came in the unlikely shape of youthful whiz-kid Erret Lobban Cord, a remarkable young entrepreneur who had been a successful car dealer before taking up the challenge of putting the moribund Auburn company back on its feet in 1924/5. The new broom didn't sweep too clean; when the thirty-one-year-old Cord acquired Duesenberg Inc, in 1926, he had sufficient perception to realise that in Fred Duesenberg the company possessed a rare talent. Instead of ousting him from the company, Cord praised him for being an 'acknowledged genius as a designer of both racing cars and high-grade passenger cars'.

'With the assistance of Fred Duesenberg,' promised Cord, 'I will build the world's best automobile, a car with superlative acceleration, speed and hill-climbing ability, pleasant to drive and safe, with maximum reliability and exceptionally long life, secured by the finest material and workmanship.' Sure enough two years later, at the December 1928 New York Automobile Salon, Cord unveiled his dream, the Duesenberg Model J. 'As beautiful as it is powerful,' enthused the automotive press, 'it has the power, acceleration and speed of a racing car together with the size, comfort, flexibility, durability and foolproofness which must be prime features of any outstanding passenger car.'

The 6876 cc Model J power unit was built by Lycoming, another company owned by Cord, to the designs of Fred Duesenberg. Its power output was claimed by its maker to be a remarkable 265 bhp, evidence of Fred Duesenberg's skill as a racing car designer. The specification included twin overhead camshafts actuating four valves per

OVERLEAF This one-of-a-kind Duesenberg from the Blackhawk Collection was originally built as a convertible coupé by Rollston and remodelled by Bohmann & Schwartz to the designs of Clark Gable, who wanted to impress Carole Lombard, whom he was courting at the time

cylinder, hemispherical combustion chambers and Ray-Day aluminium pistons, specifically designed to compensate for the expansion of the grey-iron cylinder block.

The massive forged crankshaft, running in five main bearings, was balanced both statically and dynamically and carried two sealed cartridges filled with mercury, which damped out any crank vibrations before they could be detected by the driver. The car had 15 in hydraulic brakes all round, to match its performance: 'Whether on straight road or curve the Duesenberg traces a true, steady course without the slightest pitching or sideway – even above 100 miles per hour. Due to perfect weight distribution, low centre of gravity and other factors, the car negotiates curves as though it were on rails. Here its easy, accurate steering is particularly appreciated. Curves may be taken at surprising rates of speed without the slightest skidding.

'Riding comfort such as no other car possesses is built into the new Duesenberg. Whether the pace be fast or slow, the road smooth or rough, the passengers ride with surprising ease. . . .

'To state that the maximum speed in second gear is 90 miles per hour is merely to illustrate and to emphasise the unusual superiority which distinguishes every detail of the Duesenberg automobile.'

If the performance was outstanding, the Duesenberg was years ahead of the rest of the motor industry in offering an on-board computer. This was no tangled web of high-tech electronics, however; instead, trains of precision gears housed in a 'timing box' automatically triggered lights which indicated when it was time to change the oil and service the battery. Every 75 miles, the timing box opened a spring-loaded valve which forced oil to all the chassis lubrication points. Indicator lights not only told the driver that the system was in operation, but reassured him that there was still oil in the lubricator!

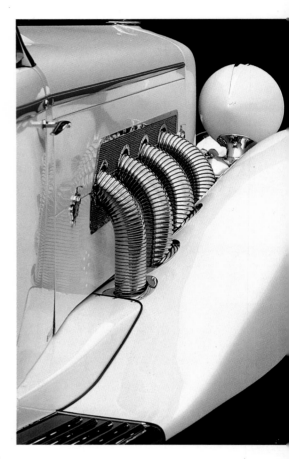

RIGHT Normally fitted to the supercharged 'SJ' Duesenbergs, the external exhaust pipes were also fitted to unsupercharged cars, like the convertible coupé owned by Clark Gable

The engine-turned nickel instrument panel of the Model J also carried 150 mph speedometer, petrol gauge, altimeter/barometer, water-temperature gauge, brake-pressure gauge, ammeter, oil-pressure gauge, tachometer, split-second stop watch, ignition control and choke and starter knobs. Cord's recipe for success was to clothe the chassis produced by his companies in beautiful bodywork: he announced that every Model J body would be custom-built to individual order. America's leading custom coachbuilders were sent blueprints of the Model J six months before it was launched and their design sketches were placed in a portfolio from which clients could choose a style which pleased them.

The clientele for the Model J was as glittering as the car itself: film stars Gary Cooper, Clark Gable, James Cagney, Greta Garbo, Joe E. Brown, Richard

ABOVE The Clark Gable Duesenberg was built on what was known as the 'JN' chassis. Gable's modifications included a lower hood line, extended bonnet, spatted rear wings and twin spare wheels at the rear

Arlen, Mae West, Lupe Velez, Marion Davies and Dolores del Rio all drove Duesenbergs; so, too, did Hollywood directors Howard Hughes, Howard Hawks and Walter Wanger. Among the crowned heads to be seen in Duesenbergs were King Alfonso of Spain, Queen Marie of Yugoslavia, Prince Serge M'Divani, the Maharajah Holkar of Indore and Prince Nicholas of Romania, who raced one of his Duesenbergs – with great enthusiasm and small success – at Le Mans.

Other celebrities who patronised the Indianapolis marque included William Randolph Hearst, the much-married millionaire Tommy Manville, bandleader Paul Whiteman, tapdancer Bill 'Bojangles' Robinson, Lew Wallace Jr (son of the author of *Ben Hur*), Mayor Jimmy Walker of New York, evangelist Father Divine, whose 178 in-wheelbase 'Throne Car' was provided by one of his female faithful,

and the President of Syria, Mehmed ben Abed.

In June 1929, a factory body-design department opened, its designers creating new body styles for individual clients and liaising between the Duesenberg company and the coachbuilder; chief designer from 1929 to 1933 was Gordon Buehrig, who subsequently achieved fame as the designer of the 'coffin-nose' Cord 810/812. Whoever fitted the bodywork, before a Duesenberg chassis was handed over to the coachbuilder, it had to pass a 500-mile test at Indianapolis.

Such perfection did not come cheap: one of the most famous Duesenbergs, built for the 1933 Chicago 'Century of Progress' exposition was a Torpedo Sedan built to Buehrig's design by Rollston of New York. Finished in platinum lacquer, the car was upholstered in heather-coloured broadcloth piped in silver leather and had burr walnut door

trim inlaid with silver. Officially named the Arlington, this supercharged Model J was more popularly known as the 'Twenty Grand' after its substantial price tag, which would equal some $800 000 today.

May 1932 saw the introduction of a supercharged Duesenberg, known as the SJ. This was built only to special order and developed 320 bhp. 'Although there are several similar sports cars manufactured in Europe,' said Duesenberg, 'they are engineered entirely for speed without regard for comfort and quietness. This new 320-horsepower Duesenberg is as quiet as the famous Model J, with the exception of a pleasant, soft singing of the supercharger, and in spite of its tremendous speed you enjoy a comfortable, safe ride.

'This supercharged Duesenberg will throttle down to three miles per hour and will accelerate from a standing start to 100 miles per hour in 20 seconds. A phaeton with top lowered has been driven at 129 miles per hour in top gear and 104 miles per hour in second gear.'

The SJ had stylish quadruple external chromed flexible exhaust pipes that were adopted by many Model J owners, too; its centrifugal supercharger turned at six times engine speed, so that at 4000 rpm, the 12 in-diameter impeller was rotating at a speed of 857 mph!

Only a few weeks after the introduction of the SJ, Fred Duesenberg, returning from a business trip in an SJ convertible coupé, skidded off the road. Although his injuries seemed slight, he collapsed and died three weeks later; he was fifty-five years old. Brother Augie became Chief Engineer of Duesenberg.

The last variation on the SJ theme came in 1936, when two short-wheelbase SS SJ roadsters were built for Hollywood stars Clark Gable and Gary Cooper.

The Duesenberg Model J was truly exclusive; just 472 chassis were built, of which thirty-six were SJ Duesenbergs. The last Duesenberg of all was an SJ, completed in 1938 — after the factory had closed down — to the order of a German enthusiast, Rudolf Bauer, who already possessed two Duesenberg phaetons.

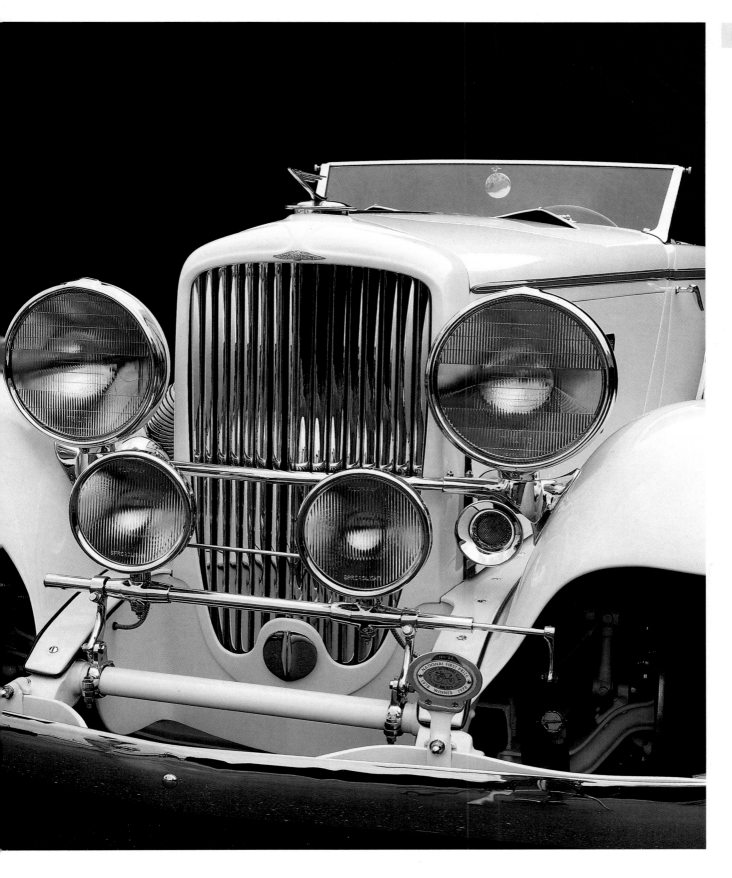

FERRARI 250 SWB/GTO

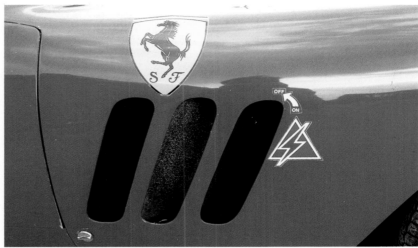

Enzo Ferrari, former racing driver and head of Alfa Romeo's racing team during the 1930s, nursed an ambition to build a sports car; it was to this end that he went into car manufacture in a new factory at Maranello, 12 miles from his native Modena, late in 1946. His first product was the 1947 Tipo 125 sports-racer, with a 1500 cc single-overhead-camshaft V12 power unit designed by Gioacchino Colombo.

Enzo Ferrari had admired V12 engines since he had first come across the American Packard Twin-Six staff cars of World War I and the Packard and Delage racing V12s of the 1920s and '30s. Colombo's complex power unit was strangled by inefficient induction arrangements, yet the car – aided by a particularly light chassis – was still capable of winning races. In any case, Colombo's able assistant, Aurelio Lampredi, redesigned the V12 to such good effect that he was given Colombo's job; Ferrari

BOTH PAGES Although the 'O' in 'GTO' signifies *omologato* (homologated), Ferrari built fewer than forty examples of the 250 GTO instead of the stipulated 100. When asked why, Ferrari replied that the car was too fast and only a few men in the world could master its performance. Spellbound, the FIA (the governing body of motor sport) homologated the 250 GTO anyway.... Amazingly, the beautiful bodywork was developed 'in house' at the Ferrari works

What is the 250GT like to drive? The quick answer is extremely exhilarating. It confirms our belief that a very fast car, properly designed and developed, is safer at normal speeds than are lesser models – and quite as safe when driven much faster.
Maurice A. Smith, 1964

never shrank from sacking designers who failed to deliver the goods. . . .

The first road-going Ferrari sports car, the 1995 cc Tipo 166, appeared late in 1947, a succession of progressively larger V12 sports cars appearing over the ensuing years. In October 1954, the 'Colombo' short-block V12 appeared in the 250GT: in the wake of the 1955 Le Mans tragedy when Levegh's Mercedes cannoned off Macklin's Austin-Healey and flew into the crowd, interest in the classic sports/racing car was curiously revived and an international Gran Turismo championship was inaugurated in 1956.

ABOVE This is the 4-litre engine of the rare 330 GTO, of which only three were built; this one was constructed to the personal specification of French Ferrari enthusiast Michel Cavallier

It was dominated from the start by the Ferrari 250GT Berlinetta, the competition version of the 250GT, with a more potent engine and bodywork stripped of its more civilised features (although it could – just – still be used on the street). The Ferrari Berlinettas dominated the ten-day Tour de France to such an extent that the long-wheelbase version became known as the 'TDF'.

Then, in 1959, a short-wheelbase 250GT, developed by Ferrari engineer Giotto Bizzarrini, appeared, with attractively stubby *berlinetta* bodywork built by Scaglietti to a Pininfarina design. It was launched, without great fanfares, at the 1959 Paris Salon, but was to prove perhaps the most successful Ferrari of all

in the way it combined good road manners with the ability to do more than hold its own on the race track.

Some 250 SWB *berlinetta*s are believed to have been built, but only about a quarter of these were the lightweight competition version, the sort that the owner could drive to the circuit and win a race with, then drive home again. Just two competition SWB Ferraris were built with right-hand drive, both were run by Rob Walker and campaigned by Stirling Moss, who took the British Empire Trophy, the Peco Trophy, the Tourist Trophy and the Nassau Tourist race in one, and came first in events which included the Redex Trophy with the other.

The first of these cars was sold to racing driver Chris Kerrison, who entered it in the 1962 Tourist Trophy at Goodwood; he was lying eighth after sixty-two laps out of one hundred when the leader, John Surtees, was put off-line by Jim Clark's Aston Martin, lying a lap behind, which spun into the ditch on the exit from a bend. Surtees went off, too, and Kerrison's car was also a victim of the incident, which, gasped *Autocar*, put 'some £15 000-worth of machinery out of the race in one blow . . .'.

Kerrison sent his damaged car to Italy for rebodying by Piero Drogo; it was now lighter and therefore more competitive, and was raced until 1967, when it was crashed in Ireland. It passed through several hands until it was acquired by confectioner Clive Beecham, who restored the Ferrari to its original appearance, with a completely new aluminium body to the original pattern and repainted in Rob Walker's dark blue livery – to such good effect that in 1986 the SWB was driven to Le Mans for the historic parade just as it would have been driven to the Sarthe circuit in 1961, when it was raced by Moss and Graham Hill.

In that same race, Ferrari entered what he referred to as a '250GT Special', which was driven by Tavano and Baghetti; it was basically a 400 SuperAmerica fitted with a

250GT engine brought up to Testa Rossa standard. Ferrari built two of these cars, and from them was developed the 250GTO – O for *Omologato* (homologated) – which has been described as 'for all intents and purposes a Testa Rossa with a roof'. Ferrari was supposed to build a hundred of these GTOs to comply with the regulations, but fewer than forty were actually constructed, because Enzo Ferrari said that it wasn't worth building more as the market for such a car was already saturated, and anyway there were not many men about who were capable of driving such a fast and ferocious car!

Like the SWB, the GTO had a strong tubular chassis, independent front suspension and a rigid rear axle, but where the SWB had looked hunched and muscular, the GTO was sleek and purposeful, perhaps the most stylish of all the Ferrari *berlinettas*. Yet it's said that no *carrozzeria* shaped its glorious lines; it was apparently styled in-house, with nothing actually being put on paper until after the first car had been completed!

Whatever the truth of that assertion, the unknown designer who fashioned the 250GTO created a masterwork. You

BELOW Cavallier's 330 GTO was, recalls former owner Martin Hilton, a superlative road car with light, positive steering and far more torque than the 3-litre car. Its shape was glorious, too

might expect a car that looked so aesthetically right to have some mechanical shortcoming; after all, don't the sages tell us that beauty is only skin deep? They are, of course, wrong: the 250GTO was famed as being ultra-reliable in its day, its gearbox was 'bullet-proof' and the handling, according to

drivers of the day, fantastic. One of the most discerning of car connoisseurs, Nick Mason, sums up his 250GTO as 'one of the most perfect cars of all time'.

For one fastidious Frenchman, Michel Cavallier, the 250GTO was not enough. Now Cavallier, a director of the French Pont-a-Mousson industrial concern, was

and a SuperAmerica chassis, which was slightly longer.

Cavallier had his car built to his own specification; recalls Martin Hilton, who owned the car for five years: 'The car was right-hand drive because Cavallier thought racing cars *should* be right-hand drive . . .'. When the 330 was delivered, Cavallier was not satisfied with the carburation, so the car was sent back to the Ferrari works for rectification. Unfortunately, while it was there, Cavallier died, so the 330GTO was offered for sale by the works.

The British concessionaire, Colonel Ronnie Hoare, was visiting Maranello, liked the car, and brought it back to England. 'Unfortunately,' recalls Hilton, 'it didn't sell very quickly, and sat in Hoare's showrooms for eight months. Eventually it was bought by a man named Daniels, who owned it for sixteen years. I bought it from him; he had never raced or rallied it, apart from a few club events: I used it rather severely for the next five years or so.'

Hilton goes on to compare his car with the 250GTO: It was an extremely good car, much more powerful than the 3-litre GTO, even though it wouldn't rev as high – it would only reach about 6500 rpm; but it had so much more torque than the 250GTO. The steering was light and positive, too.

'It was an extremely good long-distance car. I recall doing a trip from Antibes in the south of France to my home in Sussex. Including a one-hour wait for the hovercraft at Calais, it took just 12 hours door to door.'

such a good customer of Ferrari – he ordered four custom-built models – that he was made a director of SEFAC (Societá Esercizo Fabbriche Automobili e Corsa) Ferrari. In 1962, he ordered a very special car, a 330GTO; only three of these were built, superficially resembling the 250GTO, but with a 4-litre engine

BOTH PAGES The frontal aspect of the 330 GTO, with flawless lines. The supplementary nasal air intakes give the Ferrari 250 and 330 GTOs a very distinctive appearance. Yet, although the 4-litre 330 GTO was externally similar to the 3-litre 250 GTO, it was built on the slightly longer SuperAmerica chassis. The dashboard of the 330 GTO (*above left*) is a very purposeful design, dominated by the large tachometer – there is neither speedometer nor odometer. The small red needle on the tachometer dial is an indicator showing how high the engine has revved, although the 7750 rpm recorded here represent a mystery, since past owner Martin Hilton says the car could only reach 6500 rpm . . .

FERRARI TESTA ROSSA

BOTH PAGES In its heyday, this ex-works 1959 Testa Rossa was driven by Dan Gurney, Phil Hill and Wolfgang von Trips. In 1959 it was run by the factory team as a long-wheelbase car with a wet-sump engine; it was returned to the Ferrari works at Maranello at the end of that season for the chassis to be shortened and a dry-sump engine fitted

Ferrari first used the Testa Rossa name on the four-cylinder 500TR sports car of 1956, because the cylinder head was painted red. The car with which the name is normally associated, however – even the modern Pininfarina-bodied Testarossa is, after all, merely basking in the reflected glory of its eponymous ancestor – was the 250 Testa Rossa sports car which made its debut at the Nürburgring in May 1957. Not only was it a more powerful successor to the four-cylinder Testa Rossa, but its 2953 cc V12 engine was a calculated anticipation that the Commission Sportive Internationale would reduce the capacity limit for sports car championship contenders to 3 litres for 1958.

Enzo Ferrari intended the new car to be a reliable machine as the next step up for his customers who had raced the four-cylinder Testa Rossa and now wanted something with similar handling characteristics – but altogether faster. Its 250TR engine was based on the well proven single-overhead-cam 250 Gran Turismo power unit; engineer Chiti revised the cylinder head design and fitted high-compression pistons, machined con-rods and a sextet of twin-choke

Testa Rossa e nome glorioso nella storia delle corse. Richiama alla mente una 'sportiva' che diede alla Ferrari una serie di allori indimenticabili (Testa Rossa is a glorious name in motor racing history. It brings to mind a sports car which bestowed on Ferrari a series of unforgettable laurels).
Pininfarina catalogue

ABOVE Sent to the United States after the 1960 season, this Testa Rossa was fitted with a Ford stock-car engine and had its de Dion rear suspension replaced by a Ford rigid rear axle. Fortunately, it eventually came to Britain for restoration to the superlative original condition seen here

carburettors to boost the power from 220 to 300 bhp at a heady 7200 rpm.

On its debut, in the Nürburgring 1000 km sports car race, the 3-litre Testa Rossa was described as 'an interesting new sports car (with) a 250 Europa engine fitted in a chassis very similar to, though larger than, the Testa Rossa, but using a de Dion rear axle'. This was the very first of the new cars, using a 290MM chassis. In the race, it was driven by Masten Gregory and the less experienced Morolli (although Olivier Gendebien made the sixth fastest practice lap in the new car). Against stiff opposition, it finished in tenth place, having covered forty-two laps of that impossibly twisting 14-mile circuit in 7 hr 37 min 8.7 sec, an average of some 78 mph.

A few weeks later, at Le Mans, the archetypal Testa Rossa shape made its debut. Designed and built by Scaglietti,

this had neat pontoon front wings, intended to give a direct airflow on to the front brake drums – Ferrari refused to use the new-fangled discs – with cutaways behind the wheels. The engine in this case had a capacity of 3.1 litres and was 'extremely fast – while it lasted'; suspension on this car was by coil springs and live rear axle. Driven by Gendebien and Maurice Trintignant, the Testa Rossa was capable of exceeding 158 mph down the Mulsanne Straight, but was eliminated by piston failure when it was lying third in the race.

The 1957 competition history of the Testa Rossa was merely a cautious toe in the water as a prelude to 1958, the *annus mirabilis* of the model, which gave Ferrari the sports car manufacturers' championship, with victories at Buenos Aires, Sebring, the Targa Florio and Le Mans. Their main rivals, Aston Martin, won the Nürburgring 1000 km event, but it was small consolation, for, with four firsts, three seconds, two thirds and three fourth places, Ferrari took the championship by thirty-eight points to Aston Martin's sixteen – and didn't even bother to run in the last round of the championship, the Tourist Trophy.

Ferrari's galaxy of drivers that year included such names as Mike Hawthorn, Peter Collins, 'Taffy' von Trips, Olivier Gendebien, Phil Hill . . . and it was apparent that the works cars had reverted to a more conventional nasal treatment, the pretty pontoon wings proving to have fairly dubious aerodynamics. Works cars, too, tended to have de Dion rear suspension. The 250TR Ferrari was a most impressive car

however: John Bolster of *Autosport* tested a Testa on the Goodwood circuit in Sussex in 1960 and found its live axle a little inadequate for the power-to-weight ratio, which permitted wheelspin at up to 80 mph in second gear! While Bolster admitted 'I really had to work to keep this projectile on the circuit at racing speeds', he qualified this opinion by adding 'curiously enough, this exciting machine is very controllable in a "hairy way", and I found I could slide it without entering the decor . . .'

Despite its super performance, the Testa Rossa was a remarkably reliable machine, and its smooth-turning V12 engine never seemed to be over-stressed. The car dominated sports car racing to such an extent – after a poor

BELOW The first real chance the owner had to drive the car after its restoration was in the historic parade at Le Mans: 'It was so well balanced – you could put your foot down on the Mulsanne Straight and take your hands off the wheel at 100 mph – it just ran dead straight; it was fantastic!'

1959, in which the 250TRs failed to finish in the Targa Florio and at Le Mans, and only won the Sebring race, they won Le Mans and Sebring in 1960–61, and Sebring in 1962 – that it's difficult to realise just how few examples of it were actually built; just thirty-three left the Ferrari works in five years, plus one 4-litre 330TR/LM with a lengthened chassis which won Le Mans in 1962, and

nearly half of those Testa Rossas were built as works cars.

Small wonder that the last time a Testa Rossa – the 1958 ex-Ecurie Belge car, which finished sixth at Le Mans in that year – came under the hammer at auction, it fetched only a shade under a million pounds. Even though those glorious cutaway wings had been expertly faired in. . . .

BOTH PAGES The owner recalls: 'Ferrari really had the roadholding sorted out; but when we checked, we found that there was nearly half an inch toe-in on the rear wheels! The chassis is incredibly stiff – it's completely unlike the pontoon car, which has a straightforward ladder chassis like the 250. The works cars were completely different, with a space frame chassis and a full de Dion rear end, five-speed indirect box, lots of bits in Elektron . . . it's a completely different car, and it feels it!'

FORD GT40

If you have the money to buy a new conception in road motoring, you will not be disappointed; if a Jaguar, Ferrari or Aston Martin satisfies you, then the unbelievable qualities of a Ford GT40 will probably be beyond your appreciation.

Denis Jenkinson, *Motor Sport*, 1966

It all started when the Ford factory in Cologne, Germany, received a letter from the American Consul in Milan, Italy, saying that an intermediary representing a 'small, but internationally known Italian auto factory' had been in touch with them regarding a possible joint venture.

Cologne, after having ascertained that the company in question was Ferrari,

forwarded the letter to Ford's head office in Dearborn, Michigan, where Lee Iacocca, flushed with the success of the newly launched Mustang, was looking for a prestige label for Ford. He, oddly enough, was interested in buying Ferrari for their body-building prowess, which was akin to hiring John Wayne for his skill as a tap-dancer. They could do it, but they were much happier to leave it to others whose abilities were better developed.

A team of Ford fact-finders quickly descended on the Ferrari factory at Maranello, compiling a detailed inventory of all the company's assets. The deal proposed by Ferrari was simple: Ford would obtain exclusive rights to all the Ferrari products and designs, the

Perhaps the best-known racing livery for the Ford GT40 was the blue and orange of Gulf Petroleum, who backed the winning team at Le Mans in 1968/9

company's name and trademarks and ninety per cent of the equity in the parent company. Lawyers representing both sides began hammering out a deal, and as the negotiations progressed, the asking price dropped from $18 million to $10 million: Ferrari was obviously as desperate to sell as Ford was to buy.

The terms of the deal were finalised and a press conference arranged to reveal the merger to the world. Then, suddenly, Ferrari had cold feet. He could sense his supreme power over Maranello being threatened by the corporation men and broke off the deal during a night-time negotiating session, declaiming: 'My rights, my integrity, my very being as a manufacturer, as an entrepreneur, as the leader of the Ferrari works, cannot work under the enormous machine, the

suffocating bureaucracy, of the Ford Motor Company'. Less than six weeks later, he apparently had second thoughts, and tentative approaches were made to see whether Ford was interested in reopening negotiations. The answer was brief and uncompromising: 'We are not interested'.

The reason was simple: as soon as the failure of the Ferrari deal was known in Dearborn, Ford staff began working on an alternative proposal, to establish a special high-performance division with the aim of developing a car to dominate the field of endurance racing. The aim of competing in the GT prototype class was simple; there, racing cars could be competitive while employing the same power units as used in mass-produced American cars and the lessons learned in competition

BELOW Rear view of the GT40 road car, chassis 1066, which toured the US as a show car in 1965. The moulded-in tail spoiler was added after testing at Le Mans in the summer of 1965 had revealed the original body's aerodynamic instability at high speed

with regard to reducing aerodynamic drag and increasing high-speed stability could prove beneficial to the design of production cars. The ultimate goal of the project was victory in the Le Mans 24-hour race and the world constructors' championship. If Ford couldn't join Ferrari, then they were going to beat him. . . .

Named as head of the new division was Roy Lunn, a British engineer working in Dearborn who had been with Aston Martin and Jowett before joining Ford. He flew to Europe in the summer of 1963, accompanied by a couple of Ford men and Carroll Shelby, to see the Le Mans race and to find someone who could build the car they had in mind. So that the project could get under way with a minimum of delay, the Ford men took over an existing design, the sensational Lola GT shown at that year's Racing Car Show in London, and a subsidiary company, Ford Advanced Vehicles, was established at Slough, handily close to Heathrow Airport, under the management of John Wyer, a former Sunbeam apprentice who had headed Aston Martin's competition department during the great days of the 1950s.

Engineering design work started in earnest in August 1963 and on 3 April 1964 the '200 mph Ford GT' was revealed to the world's press before it was flown across the Atlantic to star in the New York Motor Show. It stood just 40 inches high, so it was known as the GT40.

Initially, the GT40, whose monocoque light-alloy chassis tub incorporated the roof panel and door cutouts, with detachable glassfibre nose and tail sections, was powered by an all-aluminium version of the Ford Fairlane 4.2-litre engine used at Indianapolis. Just eight months after the start of work on the car, the first two GT40s took part in the Le Mans trials. The Ford wind tunnel had only been able to simulate speeds of up to 125 mph, however, and on the Mulsanne Straight the cars were

considerably faster. Both Roy Salvadori and Jo Schlesser found that the Fords were exhibiting rear-end lift and after only eight laps Schlesser lost control, writing off the very first GT40. Modified aerodynamics – principally the addition across the rear of the car of a spoiler – solved the stability problem and also made the car faster.

The GT40 was entered in the Nürburgring 1000 km race, driven by Bruce McLaren and Phil Hill, but despite a good start, it was withdrawn after 213 km when chassis weakness became a problem. All three cars entered for the Le Mans 24 Hours were modified and in

BELOW The cockpit of the GT40 is stark and purposeful; many of the minor controls and gauges are production Ford items; the studs in the seats were originally intended to cool the occupants! This car is fitted with the standard 4.7-litre power unit, although the works racing MkIIs used the larger 7-litre engine, which was put out of contention after regulations changed at the end of 1967

the actual Le Mans race, the GT40 was timed on the Mulsanne Straight at 207 mph and set a new lap record of 3 min 49.2 sec (131.67 mph). However, transmission failure progressively eliminated the cars and the last of them dropped out after 11 hr 30 min, when it was lying fourth.

It was the same story in 1965, when a new 4.7-litre engine developed from that of the Fairlane 500 was first fitted to the GT40: a new lap record was set at Le Mans, but the Ford team still failed to finish. That year also saw trials start with a 7-litre version of the GT40 and by now the design had reached the stage where it could be offered for sale with some confidence, so a production line was established at Slough, where manufacture of an initial batch of fifty cars began.

In January 1966, Ford announced a road version of the GT40: it was, the company proclaimed, 'the most expensive Ford ever'; and, at £7253 including tax, it cost fifteen times as much as the cheapest Ford Anglia then available and six times as much as the flagship of the Ford range, the Mk IV Zodiac. Fitted with a detuned 4.7-litre engine, it could still reach 164 mph. However, only thirty-one of these road-going MkI GT40s were built. That year saw the 7-litre racing GT40 come to maturity, with a 1–2–3 victory at Daytona, first and second at Sebring, a classic 1–2–3 finish at Le Mans and a coveted constructors' championship for Ford.

The GT40's second Le Mans victory came in 1967, when the Sebring win was also repeated, but at the end of that season, the rules changed and Ford announced that it was withdrawing from sports-car racing. The rights to the GT40 were passsed to a newly formed

BELOW The GT40 got its name because the car stood just 40 inches high. This gave tall drivers some problems, and some of the racing cars had a curious 'bubble' moulded into the roof to overcome this difficulty

partnership, JW Automotive, in which John Willment and John Wyer were the guiding spirits. With backing from Gulf Oil (whose vice-president Grady Davis was a keen GT40 owner), the 4.7-litre cars ran in Gulf's European livery of blue with an orange dividing stripe. They won at Le Mans, the BOAC 500 at Brands Hatch, the Monza 1000 km and the Watkins Glen Endurance Race, and took the World Sports Car Manufacturers' Championship for the second time in three years.

The GT40 story really came to a cliff-hanging climax in June 1969 when Jacky Ickx drove car No 1075, (the 1968 winner) to a 100-yard victory over Herrmann's Porsche after 3123.75 miles of racing. It was the first car ever to win Le Mans twice and after the race it was retired to a museum. More recently, however, that GT40 was sold off by

Burmah Oil, after they took over Gulf, and it is now back on the track in historic events.

Ford had shown that it could beat Ferrari at his own game; total production of both road and race GT40s was around 103 cars, although in recent years a limited run of 'Mk V' GT40s has been constructed by JW Automotive, a sure sign that the car has entered the stratospheric league of motordom.

The GT40 more than fulfilled those early image-building ambitions – or, as a famous advertisement that showed a puzzled traffic warden about to book a GT40 asked: 'Would you let your daughter go out with a man who owns a Ford?'

BELOW Mean front view of the GT40, perhaps the archetypal sports/racing car of the 1960s, and certainly a very satisfactory outcome of Ford's failure to buy Ferrari!

HISPANO-SUIZA H6C

Unless you have driven the Targa Florio course in Sicily in anger, you cannot begin to comprehend the achievement of aperitif king André Dubonnet in finishing fifth in the 1924 Targa. Twisting, turning, snaking, the road loops round the Madonie mountains. There are, it's said, over two hundred corners on the Medio Madonie circuit that they used in 1924.

Yet Dubonnet drove that trying race – it was 268 miles long – in a massive wooden-bodied Hispano-Suiza with a six-cylinder engine displacing 7983 cc and scaling, even stripped for racing, over 35 cwt. You might think this to be a car more suited to the lazy ways of the *concours* field than the myriad bends of the Madonie; yet the Boulogne H6C Hispano-Suiza was a sports-racer to challenge the best the world had to offer.

The marque name means Spanish-Swiss and records the marriage of Swiss brains and Spanish cash, since the company's chief engineer and presiding genius, Marc Birkigt, was a Swiss engineer who had been persuaded to move to Barcelona at the turn of the century to join an electrical company named La Cuadra. He quickly persuaded them to back the construction of an automobile he had designed – it was Spain's first production car – but financial difficulties caused the end of production in 1901.

The chief creditor, Castro, took over, and car production was resumed under his name, but again lack of finance brought the venture to a halt. However, out of the wreckage, the far-sighted Damien Mateu created a new company, the Fabrica La Hispano-Suiza de Automovils.

Soon, Spain's 'boy-king', Alfonso XIII, bought the first Hispano-Suiza of some thirty he would own. When his young wife gave him the latest sports Hispano for his birthday, the model was named the Alfonso XIII in his honour.

The marque's fame rapidly spread beyond the borders of its homeland, to such effect that Hispano-Suiza opened an assembly plant at Levallois-Perret, Paris, in 1911 to serve its fashionable French clientele; increased demand nonetheless forced a move to a larger factory in nearby Bois-Colombes in 1914; it was the French factory which introduced the magnificent 32cv H6 series in 1919, with its light-alloy engine whose design drew its inspiration – if not its configuration – from the V8 Hispano-Suiza aero-engine which powered many of the famous fighting

BOTH PAGES This splendid Hispano-Suiza H6B was commissioned in 1929 by the Maharajah of Alwar as a wedding present for his son. The celebrated French *carrossier* Kellner built the cabriolet-roadster bodywork; despite its elegance, the car was intended for panther hunting, which is why there are spotlights either side of the windscreen. These are mounted on extensible arms so that they can be focussed on the quarry. The bell mounted ahead of the radiator was to clear natives out of the car's way . . .

Like a huge yellow insect that had dropped to earth from a butterfly civilisation, this car, gallant and suave, rested in the lowly silence of the Shepherd's Market night. Open as a yacht, it wore a great shining bonnet, and, flying over the crest of this great bonnet, was that silver stork by which the gentle may be pleased to know that they have just escaped death beneath the wheels of a Hispano-Suiza car, as supplied to His Most Catholic Majesty.

The Green Hat, by Michael Arlen, 1924

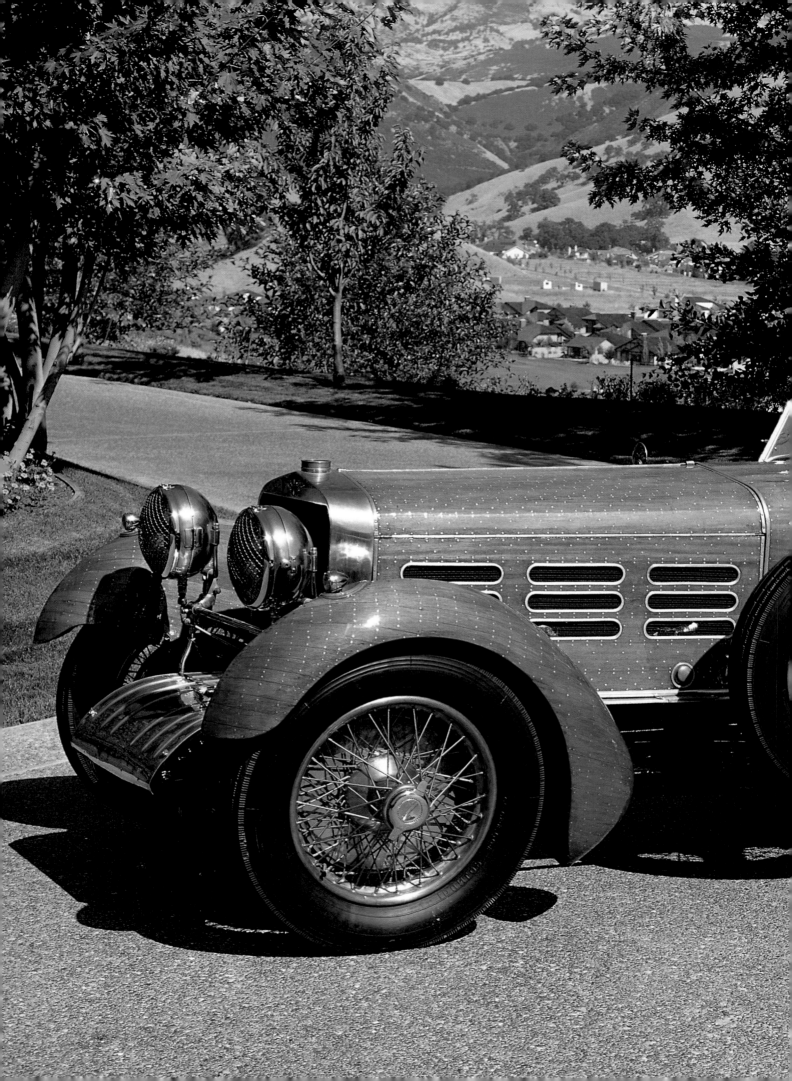

biplanes of World War I. Most particularly, the V8 Hispano had powered the SPAD combat biplane of France's 'Ace of Aces', Georges Guynemer, and to commemorate the association with the pale, consumptive Guynemer the H6 bore a flying stork mascot based on the squadron insignia of the *Escadrille Cicogne* with which he flew.

The engine of the H6 was a monobloc overhead-camshaft 6597 cc six: to match its performance, the H6 was endowed with the innovative feature of servo-assisted four-wheel braking, whose design was of such perfection that the system was adopted some years later by Rolls-Royce. The only retrograde feature was a three-speed gearbox with rather widely spaced ratios.

The Autocar commented in 1923: 'A show-finished chassis of the Hispano-Suiza sometimes strikes one not so much as a car for everyday use as a fine example of craftsmanship staged for exhibition. In fact, the Hispano is a really practical car, as any motorist who has visited France will testify. It stands, in its way, alone, because it can satisfy the "carriage folk" and the sportsman alike.'

André Dubonnet was certainly satisfied with his Hispano-Suizas, for in 1921, he and two friends drove a four-seater H6 from Paris to Nice – some 588 miles – in 12 hr 55 min, a remarkable average of 45 mph. Then Dubonnet won the Coupe Boillot race at Boulogne with an H6, averaging 65 mph against such rapid competition as the Becquet Special, an Hispano V8 aero-engine shoehorned into a 1914 Alda Grand Prix chassis.

He set the best touring-car speed in the San Sebastian race in 1922, won again at Boulogne and took first place from Count Conelli's Indianapolis 4.9-litre Ballot at Monza. The rare 6864 cc short-wheelbase sports H6, capable of exceeding 100 mph, was named Monza in honour of the victory. This was developed into the 7983 cc Boulogne, which went into production in 1923.

When Dubonnet bespoke his Boulogne, he had its bodywork built by a famous aircraft company, Nieuport Astra Aviation, who created a glorious wooden shell of copper-riveted Honduras tulipwood, which weighed a mere 170 lb. After its Targa Florio exploit, Dubonnet's Boulogne was sold to the Keiller family in Britain, thus making the bizarre change from aperitifs to marmalade. It was laid up for many years and suffered superficial damage in an air-raid on Plymouth.

In the 1950s it was restored by an enthusiast named Gerry Albertini, who had the ugly cycle wings originally fitted overlaid with riveted tulipwood by a Thames boatbuilder to match the bodywork. Since then, the car has found its way across the Atlantic, and now resides in the Blackhawk Collection in California.

The history of the H6 series Hispano provides a remarkable instance of a swan evolving into an ugly duckling: the well-known Czechoslovakian armaments firm of Skoda produced the H6B version of the Hispano-Suiza under licence from 1924 to 1927. After that, it was all anticlimax.

RIGHT & PREVIOUS PAGE The flying-stork mascot on the Hispano-Suiza, whose badge combined the flags of Spain and Switzerland, was in remembrance of the tubercular boy ace Georges Guynemer, whose SPAD fighter of the crack *Escadrille Cicogne* was Hispano-powered. And it was aviation that created the most famous H6B, for the Nieuport Astra Aviation company used aircraft constructional techniques – a monocoque structure of copper-riveted tulipwood – to build the beautiful ultra-light body of André Dubonnet's Targa Florio entry in 1924 (*previous page*)

ABOVE & LEFT One of the prettiest body styles of the mid-1920s was the boat-tailed two-seater, seen here on a 1928 Hispano-Suiza with the 45 hp Boulogne engine. The power unit of the H6 series (*left*) was based on the World War I aviation experience of Hispano-Suiza, whose marvellous overhead-camshaft V8 engines were used in the finest fighting aircraft like the SPAD and the SE5A. The nitrided-steel cylinder liners were screwed into the light-alloy cylinder block and the 99 lb seven-bearing crankshaft was machined from a 770 lb billet of steel

HISPANO-SUIZA V12

BOTH PAGES This svelte coupé on the 9425 cc J12 chassis was designed and built by Howard 'Dutch' Darrin as one of a matching pair of Hispano-Suizas: a six-cylinder K6 *coupé-chauffeur* for town use and a V12 owner-driver coupé for outstanding road performance. Darrin's client was banker Anthony Gustav de Rothschild, who took delivery of the cars in September 1934. He retained the twelve-cylinder car for 16 years, while his family kept the six-cylinder *coupé-chauffeur* for 50 years. The two cars were reunited in the Blackhawk Collection in 1984

Let's face it, the Bugatti Royale was not a commercial success; even with Ettore Bugatti's labour-intensive methods, there was no way a total production of six (or maybe seven) could have shown any sort of profit, even if all the cars had sold. However, during the same era, Hispano-Suiza built and sold a car comparable in size and grandeur to the Royale and managed to find around 110 wealthy enthusiasts willing to part with about £3500 for it (the Bugatti – always impractical – would have cost around £6500), prices which equate to £85 000 and £158 000 in today's money.

Looked at in those terms, the V12 Hispano-Suiza was really astoundingly good value for money and a far more usable car than the Bugatti. It was launched at the 1931 Paris Salon with an astonishing *coup de theatre* in which the leading French motoring journalist, Charles Faroux, drove a V12 Hispano-Suiza from Paris to Nice and back to the Hispano showrooms, where he parked the car on a huge sheet of white paper. Not one drop of oil or water leaked on to the paper. . . .

Known as the Type 68, the new Hispano arrived right at the heart of the great Depression, hardly, you might think, the ideal time to launch a luxury car. Marc Birkigt drew on his skill as a designer of aviation engines in creating the power unit, a 60-degree V12, equipped with pushrod-operated overhead valves instead of the single overhead camshaft of the H6 series. Unusually for the period, bore and stroke dimensions were 'square' at 100 mm each, giving a swept volume of 9425 cc, and as in Hispano-Suiza's aero-engines, the cylinder blocks of the Type 68 were fixed-head aluminium castings with screwed-in nitralloy liners. There were sodium-cooled exhaust valves and a nine-bearing crankshaft whose connecting rods had dove-tailed big-end caps secured by riveted pins.

Hispano-Suiza cars . . . are not drastically modified at regular intervals. They are designs which have been developed with painstaking care for a specific performance and purpose, not built to a price in the ordinary way, and are representative of the very best automobile practice and construction.

The Autocar, 1934

'Dutch' Darrin's mastery of line is shown in the three-quarter-rear view of the Rothschild coupé with its 'fastback' roofline. The car has a removable roof section above the driver's seat; the blind rear quarter panels give absolute privacy to the rear-seat occupants

138

The Type 68 was available in four chassis lengths – 135 in, 144 in, 150 in and 162 in – of which some fifty per cent was bonnet – passenger accommodation was not this car's strong point! Other weak points of the design were the three-speed transmission and poor steering lock. Nevertheless, this Hispano was outstanding as a driver's car: 'It is', exulted *The Autocar*, 'a car of which a true perspective cannot possibly be measured in a few words . . . the point of the car, apart from its acceleration, is not just that it is capable of a genuine 100 miles an hour . . . really is that there is no effort whatever, even when the car is travelling

at its limit speed.' Of course, there was a penalty for such performance, and that was a fuel consumption of 10 mpg – but with petrol at around 2 shillings (10 p) a gallon, maybe that wasn't important. . . .

The Type 68 was developed into the magnificent 68 *bis*, with the engine enlarged to 11 310 cc and the term 'supercar', now so widely used, was coined to describe this amazing machine. Tested in 1959 by Ronald Barker of *The Autocar*, the 1934 Saoutchik-bodied Type 68 *bis* owned by Peter Hampton proved 'as quiet as a club library', and, although its high bottom gear – a 50 mph ratio – ruled out scorching acceleration from rest, once

the car was rolling its performance was truly remarkable. It took, for instance, just 10.1 seconds to accelerate from 70 to 90 mph in 'incomparably unobtrusive' style.

Passenger and luggage space was at a premium in this 211 in long car, for it was definitely a two-seater, and since the long boot was comprehensively filled with the spare wheel there was not really room for more luggage than a spongebag.

Like the power unit of the Bugatti Royale, the Type 68 Hispano-Suiza engine was also used to power high-speed railcars operated by the French National Railways. Seventy-nine of these railcars were built and they were even briefly tried in England.

Around the same time that the Type 68 *bis* appeared, Hispano-Suiza also launched a 5180 cc six-cylinder version of the Type 68; this was the K6, first shown in 1934. However, the French Hispano-Suiza factory stopped car production in 1938 to concentrate on the more lucrative business of making armaments and aero-engines in the preamble to World War II. The Barcelona plant continued car production longer, despite

the effects of the Spanish Civil War, and between 1932 and 1943 built a series of six-cylinder Hispano-Suizas. The last new model from Barcelona was the depressing T60RL, launched in 1934, which had servo-assisted Lockheed hydraulic brakes and central gear-change.

Although the output of Hispano-Suiza in Barcelona after the Spanish Civil War was negligible, the factory did have one last spell of glory: the Pegaso truck firm took over the factory in the 1940s, and built the magnificent Pegaso car there between 1951 and 1957. The last word from Bois-Colombes was not so impressive. After the war, the French factory built a front-wheel-drive prototype , powered by a Ford V8 engine, but the model failed to reach production. The post-war climate was not right for a new luxury car and the death of Marc Birkigt in 1953, at the age of seventy-five, meant that Hispano-Suiza, now profitably engaged in building aircraft components such as hydraulic landing gear, had no further inspiration to build 'cars magnificent', even though they now owned the Bugatti works as well.

LEFT & OVERLEAF Like the H6 power unit, the 9425 cc engine of the Hispano-Suiza V12 had fixed-head light-alloy cylinder castings with screwed-in nitrided steel-alloy liners. With a maximum power output of 220 bhp at a leisurely 3000 rpm, it could move the fastback coupé (*overleaf*) from 0 to 60 mph in 12 seconds and enabled it to attain a maximum speed in the region of 108 mph in arrogant defiance of the laws of aerodynamics

ISOTTA FRASCHINI

Historians remember that the Tipo 8 Isotta Fraschini was the first straight-eight car to go into series production; the world remembers that slightly faded Isotta Fraschini landaulette driven by Erich von Stroheim, playing chauffeur Max to Norma Desmond (Gloria Swanson) in the film *Sunset Boulevard*. Whatever the memory, the Tipo 8 is the stuff of which motoring dreams are made.

The lure of the Tipo 8, indeed, was enough to tempt silent-screen superstar Rudolph Valentino away from his favourite Voisins: he ordered two Isottas, a Fleetwood-bodied *coupé de ville* and a Castagna roadster, but died following an

The great and marvellous power of its engine, combined with perfect freedom from any mechanical noise, the simplicity and beauty of its design, and the extraordinary ease of its control have placed the Isotta Fraschini pre-eminent amongst the world's most exclusive automobiles.

Isotta Fraschini advertisement, 1924

unsuccessful operation before the roadster could be delivered. The car survives in the Blackhawk Collection in California, still bearing Valentino's personal mascot, a coiled cobra, which was a present from Douglas Fairbanks and Mary Pickford.

The designer of the Tipo 8 Isotta, Giustino Cattaneo, was described as a *brillante tecnico*; he was also unscrupulously ambitious, for early on in his career at Isotta Fraschini (based in Milan's Via Monterosa), Cattaneo managed to oust their brilliant but self-effacing designer Giuseppe Stefanini and take over the top engineering job. During World War I, Cattaneo experimented with prototypes intended for post-war production, and was said to have put an eight-cylinder car on the road as early as 1916. With a keen eye for the vital export markets – particularly America – he

LEFT & OVERLEAF Some of the finest coachwork of the period was fitted to the Tipo 8A Isotta Fraschini chassis. Compare the gloriously lithe boat-tailed Le Baron coupé on this page with the equally flamboyant Tipo 8A SS special sports tourer by Carrozzeria Castagna shown overleaf. Despite the fact that the Castagna car carries Rudolf Valentino's coiled-cobra mascot, it dates from 1930. The pontoon-shaped running boards double as tool boxes. Known to Americans as a dual-cowl phaeton, this body has the unusual feature of a separate windscreen for the rear seat passengers even though the car has only two doors

decided to concentrate on the one luxury straight-eight model.

Cattaneo had little previous experience to draw upon in designing the Tipo 8, which he thought of as two four-cylinder units in tandem, despite the light-alloy cylinder block being a single casting. Disregarding Isotta Fraschini's long heritage of building overhead-camshaft power units, Cattaneo specified pushrod-operated overhead valves for his new engine; he was fully up with fashion, however, in fitting aluminium pistons and a nine-bearing crankshaft with full pressure lubrication.

The power output of 80 bhp at 2200 rpm, from 5902 cc, was scarcely remarkable for 1919; Cattaneo had designed the engine for reliable service rather than out-and-out performance. Like the other outstanding new model of 1919, the H6 Hispano-Suiza, the Tipo 8 Isotta Fraschini was hampered by a three-speed gearbox, although, again like the Hispano, the new Isotta had four-wheel servo brakes. Ultimate performance had not been Cattaneo's goal, however, in designing the Tipo 8, which, equipped with the most sybaritic coachwork available, scaled over two tons ready for

the road; his aim was to achieve 'il massimo della perfezione e dell'eleganza'. According to those with experience of the model, it handles like a truck and compares badly with its contemporaries like the Hispano-Suiza H6 or the Rolls-Royce Silver Ghost; but then the Isotta was designed to be driven by a chauffeur and dynamic qualities were not paramount in its creation.

The death of the company's founding father, Oreste Fraschini, in 1921 drove the firm into financial difficulties such that it had to be totally reorganised the following year by a new group. This group launched the Tipo 8 in America, where sales were handled by the son of the one-eyed Italian poet, patriot and aviator, Gabriele d'Annunzio. It found an eager clientele, including newspaper magnate William Randolph Hearst, heavyweight boxer Jack Dempsey, and film star Clara Bow, the 'It' girl, as well as Valentino.

American sales were said to have amounted to some 450 cars (out of a total production of just under 1400 cars in the period 1919–36). In 1924 the company had agencies in London, Paris, Brussels, Madrid, Basle, New York, Buenos Aires, Sao Paolo (Brazil) and

Santiago (Chile); two-thirds of all production was exported.

In 1924, Isotta Fraschini brought out the 7372 cc Tipo 8A to counter criticism of the Isotta's performance. With a top speed approaching 90 mph, larger-diameter brakes, with Dewandre vacuum-servo assistance, were essential and a higher final drive ratio advisable.

Initially sold only in chassis form, to be fitted with bespoke bodywork by such *carrozziere* as Cesare Sala, Castagna, Ghia and Farina, from late 1928 the Tipo 8A was available with factory-built coachwork. There was a catalogued sports version, the Tipo 8ASS (Super Spinto), launched in 1926, with an increased compression ratio (5:5:1), larger valves with double springs and revised carburation contributing to a power output of some 135 bhp and a guaranteed top speed of 100 mph.

The Depression virtually wiped out the car side of Isotta Fraschini, which also built marine and aviation engines, and the company proposed a merger with Ford, anxious to expand in Italy and thwarted by Fiat (backed by Mussolini). Not for the first time, the Italian dictator vetoed the move and Isotta Fraschini was left in a parlous state. Nevertheless, in April 1931, three months after the Ford venture had been dropped, Isotta Fraschini announced the 100 mph Tipo 8B, an improved version of the Tipo 8A with a more massive chassis and an engine cast from nickel-iron, with ignition by Bosch coil instead of magneto.

Riding comfort was improved by smaller wheels with bigger (20 in x 7 in) Pirelli tyres plus longer, flatter springs controlled by double hydraulic dampers. While the three-speed gearbox was still standard, a four-speed Wilson pre-selector transmission became available as an option and was standardised towards the end of 8B production. This was purely nominal after 1932, when a new board headed by aviation engineer Giovanni Caproni took over and reduced Isotta

Fraschini's capital from 90 million lire to 9 million. Just thirty of the 8B Isotta Fraschinis were built between 1931 and the end of production, which came some five years later.

The company survived by building power units and diesel trucks, boosted by Mussolini's invasion of Ethiopia in 1936. After World War II, in which the Isotta factory was badly damaged by Allied bombing, Fabio Luigi Rapi designed a new, rear-engined Tipo 8C, which had only the number of cylinders in common with the earlier Tipo 8 models. With all-independent rubber suspension and a rear-mounted V8 engine of either 2544 cc or 2981 cc, the 8C Monterosa was short-lived; a mere 20 pre-production cars were built – and none was sold before Isotta Fraschini went into liquidation in 1949.

The name was taken over by the Costruzione Revisione Motori, and continues today on marine diesel engines, a curious fate for a marque which was once reckoned among the greatest of luxury cars. . . .

LEFT The chauffeur's compartment of the Tipo 8A landaulette emphasizes the 'upstairs downstairs' contrast, with the front seats trimmed in leather while the rear seats have soft cloth upholstery. But there is a concession to staff comfort – the panel above the division window conceals a pull-out cover for the driver's seat

BOTH PAGES The Castagna-bodied Isotta Fraschini Tipo 8A SS special sports tourer is powered by a high-performance version of Cattaneo's straight-eight power unit, with high-compression pistons, larger valves, special carburettor and intake manifold, although the standard Tipo 8A power unit (*below*) fitted to the landaulette is an impressive enough piece of engine architecture

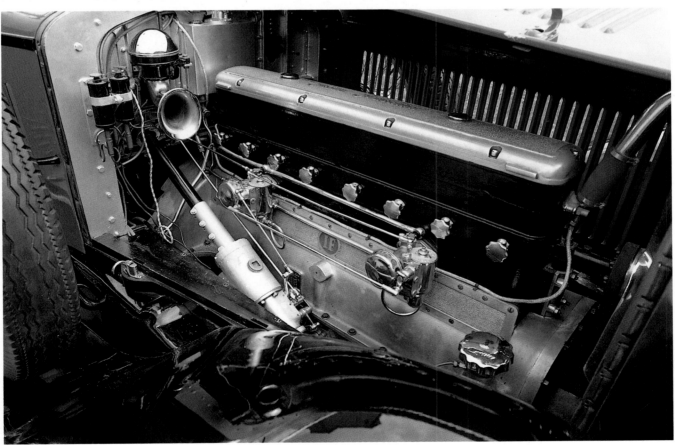

JAGUAR XK-SS

The Jaguar XK-SS is a true-blue sports car, in so much as it has racing characteristics with touring equipment. As such, it naturally has much more performance, safety and appeal than the run of sports cars.

Charles Haywood, *The Autocar*, 1957

ABOVE The history of racing cars is often confusing: XKD505, the 1955 Le Mans-winning D-type, was cannibalized by the factory to rebuild the ex-works XKD601, so there are now *two* cars which can claim to be the 1955 winner. And this car, which combines components of XKD505 and 601, is one of them

It was with the best intentions that Jaguar said they were going to build a hundred D-types to meet the new regulations for cars of over 2.5 litres, introduced by the Automobile Club de l'Ouest, organisers of the 24-hour race at Le Mans, for the 1956 event. After all, Jaguar had already won the Sarthe classic three times, in 1951 – a classic first-time-out victory for the new C-type (the 'C' stood for 'competition', the car being a racing development of the XK120) – 1953 and 1955.

For 1954, a new racing Jaguar had appeared, this time with a monocoque body shell, the first time that the Coventry marque had used this form of construction. As a natural progression from C-type, Jaguar's experimental and competition departments named the new model D-type when it was under development in the spring of 1954. Just six D-types were built during 1954 and a second place at Le Mans behind a 5-litre Ferrari showed the potential of the new model. Jaguar boasted that a considerable demand from private owners resulted from their successful performance at Le Mans and Reims, but the truth was that the change in regulations for the 1955 Le

Mans had compelled the setting up of a production line for the model in the Jaguar works at Browns Lane, Coventry in the summer of 1955. The first two pre-production models were delivered in May of that year to David Murray's Edinburgh-based private team, Ecurie Ecosse, followed by a single car for Belgium and then the four team cars (plus a spare) to be campaigned by the Jaguar

works. It was only once these eight cars had been built that the first true production D-type was completed – and exported to California.

The 1954 D-types had been of true integral construction, with the tubular front sub-frame which carried the 3442 cc twin-cam six-cylinder engine and double-wishbone independent front suspension welded to the magnesium-

ABOVE This is a 'long-nose' D-type, which, although it carries the number plate of the car (XKD601) that Duncan Hamilton crashed heavily at Le Mans in 1958, nevertheless incorporates a fair amount of the 1955 Le Mans winner, XKD505. The white intake surround identified the 1955 winner, driven by Mike Hawthorn and Ivor Bueb

Originally built as XKD569, this car was subsequently converted to XKSS713 and sold to James Peterson, builder of California's Riverside Raceway. After a chequered history, the XK-SS was acquired by film star Steve McQueen

alloy centre section; the rear bulkhead formed the attachment points for the rear suspension. However, the welded construction had proved expensive to repair, so the 1955 models had the subframe and centre section bolted together.

The beautifully flowing lines of the D-type's light-alloy bodywork were designed by Malcolm Sayer, formerly an aerodynamicist with Bristol Aeroplanes: its efficiency had been demonstrated by a

mildly-modified prototype which touched virtually 180 mph in a timed run on the Jabbeke autoroute in Belgium in late 1953. Disc brakes, with three pads on the front and two at the back to give a 60/40 braking bias, were a pioneering feature of the D-type – and, with that level of performance, a necessary one.

The 1955 Le Mans race should have been a close-fought duel between Jaguar, Mercedes and Ferrari, but in the third hour of the race the French driver Pierre

Levegh's Mercedes, travelling at 150 mph, hit the back of Lance Macklin's Austin-Healey, swerving to avoid Mike Hawthorn's D-type (which was pulling into the pits) and hurtled through the air into the crowd like a fire-bomb, killing more than eighty spectators. When the death-toll was announced in the small hours of the morning, the Mercedes factory at Stuttgart instructed the two surviving Mercedes to retire as a mark of respect for the victims. The D-type of Hawthorn and Bueb ran steadily on to win the race, but it was a hollow victory.

The 1956 event was won by the Ecurie Ecosse D-type driven by Ron Flockhart and Ninian Sanderson, after two works cars had crashed in drizzle five minutes from the start, and the Scottish team achieved a Le Mans hat-trick with a further victory in 1957.

Despite this remarkable run of success, Jaguar had been finding it an uphill struggle to sell the production D-types, priced at

£3878 in the UK (to put that into perspective, the cheapest real car on the market then was the Ford Popular at £413 and the Rolls-Royce Silver Cloud cost £918 more than the D-type). Jaguar's decision in October 1956 to withdraw from racing can hardly have helped to stir the sluggish sales of the D-type. So in late January 1957 the company announced a 'new super-performance roadster', known as the XK-SS and initially destined for export only. They claimed that the XK-SS was 'closely related' to the D-types; in fact, it was a simple conversion of the unsold racers, intended to clear the backlog of cars in stock, and the addition of better trim, a proper windscreen, hood and sidescreens and the elimination of the central strip dividing the driver's seat from that of the nominal Le Mans passenger hardly disguised its true origins. Nor, with a grid on the tail as the only luggage accommodation, could the XK-SS truly be classed as a practical touring car.

The initial batch of cars was intended for export to the United States and the first one, painted Sherwood Green, was shipped to New York around 20 January aboard the SS *America*. Jaguar cheerily announced that a revival in export business had enabled them to put the factory back on a full five-day week, but a fortnight later, that factory was gutted by a fire which destroyed 270 cars, including five XK-SSs, and cost the company an estimated £3.5 million. At that point, just sixteen XK-SSs had been built and all but one had gone to America, the exception being a car for arch-enthusiast Colonel Ronnie Hoare. Total production of the D-type/XK-SS was eighty-seven cars, and in the aftermath of the fire, when Jaguar workers were doggedly getting the factory back into production, nobody noticed that the thirteen examples needed to bring D-type output to the promised one hundred were never built.

Some of the XK-SSs, indeed, had had previous existences as D-types: car XKD569 had been tested in its D-type guise at the Motor Industry Research Association's Warwickshire test circuit in December 1955 and been signed off for stock, from which it was retrieved for conversion into XKSS713 in February 1957. It was shipped to the States and delivered to James Peterson, the man in charge of building the new Riverside Raceway. Somewhere in the early history of the car, so the story goes, is a severe case of the eternal triangle, for an early owner – history does not seem to record his name – was gunned down by his wife's

lover three months after buying the XK-SS. We're on firmer ground with the next owner, for it was film actor and motorcycle fanatic Steve McQueen, who drove the car for some 30 000 miles before 'selling' it for a token amount to the Harrah Collection, then the world's largest (and all but vanished today), to avoid his ex-wife getting her hands on it in an acrimonious divorce action.

That was in the 1960s, and by the time McQueen came to take back his car, Harrah had died, his biggest creditors

LEFT & FAR LEFT The XK-SS is clearly a mildly converted race car, with few concessions to creature comfort. To supplement the meagre luggage capacity, a grid was fitted above the tail (*far left, above*), while extra space could be made by leaving the spare wheel behind and using soft bags in the empty wheel well in the tail. A contemporary road tester noted that potential passengers needed to have short legs, because footroom in the well was so limited, but added: 'It is surprising how small an enthusiast can make himself when offered a ride in a car like this Jaguar!' The 3.4-litre Jaguar overhead-camshaft six gave the XK-SS staggering performance, with a top speed of around 145 mph available on the standard back axle ratio and the ability to reach 120 mph from rest in under 20 seconds!

BOTH PAGES Unlike the racing D-type, which just had a 'Jaguar' transfer on the nose so as not to interfere with the car's aerodynamic qualities, the XK-SS bore an elaborate 'Jaguar XK-SS' script. Underlining the limited-production aims of Jaguar for this model, these scripts were hand-made by the company's apprentices. The instrumentation (*below*) of the XK-SS is restricted to the bare essentials: speedometer and rev counter to the left of the steering wheel, oil-pressure gauge and coolant temperature gauge to the right

Holiday Inns were selling off his vast collection to clear their indebtedness, and all trace of the informal deal struck a few years earlier had vanished; so McQueen had to dig deep in order to recover what was really his rightful property. After McQueen's death, his friend and neighbour Richard Freshman bought the car at an auction of the star's effects, where fortunately, there was little competitive interest in the machine.

The Jaguar was superficially good, but a certain amount of McQueen's customising had to be removed and some body damage repaired – like the holes drilled in the box-sections by an overenthusiastic customs man involved in combating drug smuggling across the US-Mexico border. The XK-SS made the return trip to England, where it was restored over a two-year period by Lynx Engineering of Sussex, who featured the car on their stand at the 1987 London Motorfair.

The XK-SS must have had the thinnest veneer ever of civilization applied to an ostensibly roadgoing car; small wonder that over the years some of that exclusive 'production' run of sixteen cars have been converted into D-types; but then the balance has been maintained by some D-types which have, like XKD569/XKSS713, been transformed into XK-SS guise. After the almost legendary one-off XJ13 racer, the XK-SS is the rarest Jaguar of them all.

LUNAR ROVER

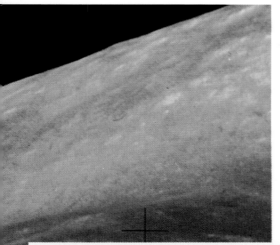

Sheer performance was hardly the prime criterion in the specification of the most expensive car ever built, for its top speed was just over 10 mph, its theoretical range 57 miles; but that car, the Lunar Roving Vehicle – the production run of four vehicles cost $19 million – had to be capable of running reliably 250 000 miles from home in temperatures ranging from 250 degrees Fahrenheit (121°C) to minus 250 degrees Fahrenheit (−157°C), with gravity one-sixth that of Earth and in zero atmosphere.

BOTH PAGES Apollo 17 commander Eugene A. Cernan test-drives the Lunar Roving Vehicle (*far left*) at the start of the first 'extra-vehicular activity' (or journey) from the mission's landing site at Taurus-Littrow on 11 December 1972. Astronaut Charles H. Duke, Jr (*left*), lunar-module pilot of the Apollo 16 mission, stands beside the Lunar Roving Vehicle at Station No 4, near Stone Mountain, during the second LRV trip from the Descartes Landing Site

There's a fundamental truth to our nature: man must explore. And this is exploration at its greatest.

Spacecraft Commander David R. Scott

The Lunar Rover project started back in 1969, when the contract to build four of these LRVs was awarded to the Boeing Company, with the first due to fly to the Moon in 1971; the contract was completed in the remarkable time of 17 months, thanks to the extensive background research that had taken place before work started.

For instance, General Motors' Delco Electronics Division, which built most of the moving parts of the LRV, had already effectively reinvented the wheel in designing a tyre that would stand up to the unique environment on the moon, where a conventional pneumatic rubber tyre would be as fragile as glass. The Delco wheel – a prototype was in existence in 1966 – was woven from piano wire and shaped to form a tyre body mounted on a spun aluminium wheel disc. In each wheel there were 64 000 precisely made intersections of the wire, which then had titanium tread strips rivetted on in a herringbone pattern to enable the LRV to cross soft ground without sinking in.

Power came from a 0.25 hp electric motor at each wheel, driving a 'wave generator' (a set of out-of-round rollers) inside a 'flexspline', a tube whose thin wall flexed as the wave generator turned inside it, enabling a 158-tooth gear on the outside of the flexspline to engage with a 160-tooth ring gear fixed to the wheel. This gave a one-step reduction of 80:1, against the three-stage gearing needed by a conventional drive, and was typical of the ingenious ways in which weight was saved on the Lunar Rover, which unladen scaled 460 lb (equivalent to a mere 76 lb on the moon).

The two/four-wheel steering (a separate servo-motor controlled each axle), speed controller and drum brakes were all operated by a single T-handle,

RIGHT Astronaut James B. Irwin salutes the specially stiffened Stars and Stripes planted in the Moon's surface by the Apollo 15 mission towards the end of the second journey by the Lunar Roving Vehicle; in the centre of the picture is the lunar module *Falcon*

which could be used by either of the two-man crew, who before the mission trained on a terrestrial version of the LRV, specially constructed to give a similar performance under Earth gravity as the real Lunar Rover would offer on the Moon.

The first LRV flew to the Moon aboard Apollo 15, which took off from Cape Kennedy on 26 July 1971 and went into lunar orbit in the afternoon of 29 June. On the following day, the Falcon lunar module separated from the Endeavour command module and made moonfall in

ABOVE Another view of the Apollo 16 mission; the Delco wheels of the Lunar Roving Vehicle were spun from piano wire, with 64,000 precisely made intersections in each wheel, which had titanium treads, enabling the vehicle to cross soft ground without sinking in the ineptly named Marsh of Decay (for the Moon has neither marshes nor decay) at 6.15 pm with Spacecraft Commander David Scott and Lunar Module Pilot James Irwin on board. Just 2 hours later, Scott surveyed the moonscape through the Falcon's hatch, describing the gently rolling terrain that lay all around for the benefit of the millions of television viewers back on Earth who were watching the Moon mission.

Early on the following morning, the two astronauts laboriously unshipped the Lunar Rover and at 11.19 am the first-ever drive on the Moon was under way, with Scott at the helm. 'The Rover handles quite well,' he reported. 'We're moving at, I guess, about eight kilometres an hour.' Scott added that the LRV was quite manoeuvrable, and that there was no tendency for dirt to collect inside the woven wire wheels.

When the LRV made its first halt, to enable the astronauts to collect samples, take photographs and make geological surveys, the LRV's on-board television camera sent back pictures to Earth, commanded by the Houston Mission Control. It was a unique co-operative effort by Detroit's two major car makers, for while it was a General Motors subsidiary that had largely built the LRV, Mission Control was built and manned by Ford personnel....

Laden with six bags of rocks, four bags of lunar soil and two core samples from the Moon's surface, Scott and Irwin drove back to Falcon. The following day saw them undertake a more ambitious journey – what the astronauts referred to as 'an extra-vehicular activity' – and they made the first lunar test of the LRV's front-wheel steering (on the first trip, it had been steered by the rear wheels): 'It works like a charm!' said Scott.

This time, the Lunar Rover covered nearly 8 miles, and sixteen bags of rock samples, eight bags of soil, six large rocks and a core sample were collected. The astronauts also found time to plant the

American flag, stiffened by wire as though blowing in a breeze that it would never feel on the airless surface of the moon.

On 2 August, Lunar Rover made its third and last trip, covering 7.8 miles along the rim of a lunar rift known as Hadley Rill and returning to base at 9.42 am. Its odometer showed that it had travelled a total of some 17.5 miles on its three 'extra-vehicular activities'. It would not be returning to earth, so its final parking place had to be carefully chosen. A little under 14 hours later, Falcon lifted off in a

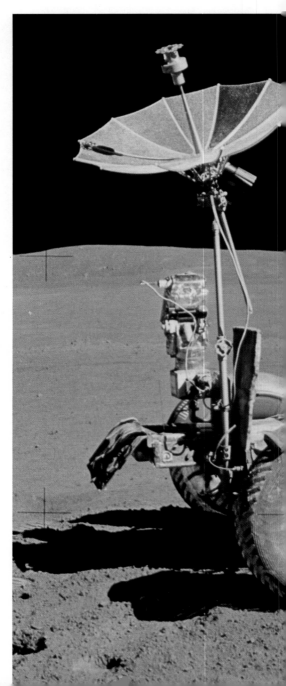

colourful shower of sparks, 'watched' for all the world by the Lunar Rover's earth-controlled camera, the first time a lunar lift-off had been televised. The dust from Falcon's wake settled quickly, leaving the LRV to its lonely vigil.

In 1972 Lunar Rovers also flew on Apollo 16 and 17 – the latter being the final Apollo mission – collecting samples and enabling the astronauts to conduct a range of experiments to discover more about the nature of the Moon.

It was during the Apollo 16 mission that the lunar speed record was established, when astronauts Young and Duke hurtled across the Moon's landscape at a heady 10.5 mph! In all, the three Lunar Rovers covered a total of some 60 miles, representing a cost of some $320,000 a mile. On the positive side of the equation, however, is the fact that there is no decay on the Moon, so that if some future moonshot needs surface transport, all the astronauts should need to do is couple up a fresh battery pack and drive away into the earthset. . . .

The Lunar Roving Vehicle pauses during its third trip on the Moon's surface during the Apollo 15 mission, looking north towards Mount Hadley, which rises some 14 765 ft above the lunar plain

MAYBACH

Among the cars that fulfil the primary needs of top speed, maximum comfort and utmost safety, the Maybach is the leader. . . .

Maybach statement, 1929

First shown at the 1938 Berlin Salon, this short-wheelbase Maybach Zeppelin V12 carries Cabriolet Sport coachwork by Spohn of Ravensburg, who bodied virtually every Maybach from the start of production in 1921

If you had to name the greatest engineers in the hundred-year history of the motor car, Wilhelm Maybach would have to be near the head of the list, for not only was he the self-effacing genius behind Gottlieb Daimler's 1886 *motorwagen*, but he also designed the epochal 1901 Mercédès, the first truly modern motor car.

Maybach resigned from the Daimler Motoren Gesellschaft in 1907, and joined his old friend Graf Ferdinand von Zeppelin to design airship engines, but it was Wilhelm's son Karl who really capitalized on the family name, by opening a factory at Friedrichshafen, close to the Zeppelin works on Lake Constance, to build aero-engines of his own design. This works, which went into action in 1912, also made marine engines and motorcycle power units and when the manufacture of aero-engines was proscribed after World War I, a side-valve 5738 cc six-cylinder car engine was put into production. However, the only customer who could be found was the low-volume luxury Dutch car builder Spyker, so Maybach decided to produce his own marque of car and the Maybach W3 first appeared in 1921.

Karl Maybach was obsessed with the concept of making driving foolproof: he felt that the driver should never need to take his hands from the wheel, so the original Maybachs had a two-speed pedal-controlled gearbox offering 'mountain gear' and 'normal' ratios. These were also the first German production cars to have four-wheel brakes and, even in the runaway inflation of Weimar Germany, Maybach managed to sell this high-quality chassis, which was clothed in custom

bodywork from Germany's top coachbuilders.

In 1926, Maybach introduced the W5, with an overhead-valve 6995 cc engine, capable of 75 mph. Maybach claimed that his concerns were with luxury and flexibility of operation rather than sheer speed, but nevertheless the Maybach company co-operated with the ZF gear works to produce the W5SG, fitted with a *Schnellgang* auxiliary two-speed overdrive which boosted top speed to 85 mph.

Maybach was, however, aiming for the ultimate in luxury and he felt that the six-cylinder engine lacked sufficient status, so in 1929 he launched the 6922 cc V12 DS7 (for Double Six 7 litres). The company's publicity for this car boasted that the design of its twelve-cylinder engine was rooted in the huge 515 hp Maybach power units supplied to the airship LZ127 *Graf Zeppelin*, which had just successfully completed a sensational round-the-world voyage.

The DS7 rode on a 147 in wheelbase, and its size dictated that its drivers needed an omnibus licence. Its engine, with cast-iron cylinder heads on light-alloy cylinder blocks, had an eight-bearing crankshaft and developed 150 bhp at 2800 rpm. The DS7 could go from walking speed to 100 mph in top gear and the *Schnellgang* was engaged simply by lifting your throttle foot, touching a vacuum control button on the steering wheel and accelerating.

This overdrive, which operated on all three of the forward speeds, was fitted under licence by Mercedes-Benz; in 1930 came a *Doppelschnellgang*, a four-speed overdrive gearbox, which was eagerly adopted by, of all unlikely licencees, the British sports car manufacturer Lagonda, looking for a way to boost the flagging sales of their 3-litre model. However, the 'box – whose complex vacuum-servo controls were selected by two small levers on the steering wheel boss – was

BOTH PAGES Priced at almost double the cost of the Mercedes-Benz 540K, the Maybach Zeppelin DS8 was the costliest car on the German market and was so large that its drivers needed to hold an omnibus licence. The monstrous V12 engine (*below*) was finished with the meticulous attention to detail that typified the aviation industry in which Maybach had its roots

so heavy that the Lagonda chassis had to be strengthened to take it.

The engine capacity of the double-six was enlarged to 7922 cc in 1931 and the 8-litre Maybach — naturally known as the DS8 — was additionally christened 'Zeppelin' in honour of its manufacturer's contribution to Germany's engineering triumph. Its engine now developed 200 bhp, but in truth this was necessary to cope with the car's massive weight: the engine alone was said to weigh a ton, the bare chassis weighed 4600 lb and a coachbuilt limousine turned the scales at a terrifying 7200 lb without passengers. Luxury features included built-in four-wheel jacks and a tyre pump and before long, a few extra ounces of deadweight were added in the shape of a model airship on the badge bar. This heavily-laden automotive pachyderm could hit

100 mph on the road – small wonder that its massive brakes were vacuum-servo assisted and that the braking assistance increased in proportion to the speed!

At first, the DS8 had a five-speed vacuum-controlled transmission, but from 1938, all examples had seven-speed gearboxes. The bulk of the Zeppelins built were bodied by Maybach's favourite coachbuilder, Spohn of Ravensberg, some 12 miles from Friedrichshafen, a few of these cars being fitted with full-width Spohn aerodynamic bodywork built to the designs of Paul Jaray. This streamlined, if ugly, coachwork was also available on the overhead-camshaft six-cylinder SW series, which was current from 1934 to 1940, but it was a more conventional Jaray streamliner on the Maybach chassis that was among Paul Jaray's own favourite executions of his aerodynamic ideals.

The first two Zeppelins were sent to Paris to be bodied by Saoutchik for the 1931 Paris Salon, but to judge from the press reports the DS8 was somewhat overshadowed by the other German V12 on show, the new 6-litre Horch, and the show cars failed to sell. They were then sent to New York in the hope that they might sell there, but Depression-hit America was not the best place to promote a huge, superluxury car, so eventually the Zeppelins were returned to Germany and rebodied by Spohn.

Money, it seemed, was of little consequence to Maybach, for the DS8, at 40 000–42 000 Reichsmarks, was too expensive for the market to bear. The Mercedes 540K was regarded as Germany's premier car, yet the 540K special roadster cost only 28 000 Reichsmarks – the price of a Zeppelin would have been sufficient not only to buy the Special Roadster, but to purchase a 540K chassis as well....

Karl Maybach's search for automotive perfection meant that his cars were hand-built and that production was slow. Consequently in the eighteen years during which he built cars, only 2300 cars left

BELOW Although the Maybach Zeppelin rose on massive 700/750x20 truck-size tyres, these were only just capable of coping with its great weight and performance

Maybach's Friedrichshafen works. The protected nature of the production of such prestige cars is shown by the fact that only a third of the Maybachs built were destined for private owners; many of the rest were used as staff cars during the war. Out of that overall production figure, some three hundred were Zeppelins and of those a mere dozen were sold in Germany; the rest were exported.

There's a neat twist to the Maybach story; the company, which continued to build specialised engines after car production had ended, was taken over by Mercedes-Benz in 1966, fifty-nine years after old Wilhelm Maybach had resigned from the company whose fame he had helped to make to go into business under his own name. The fate of the two companies, it seems, was inextricably linked. . . .

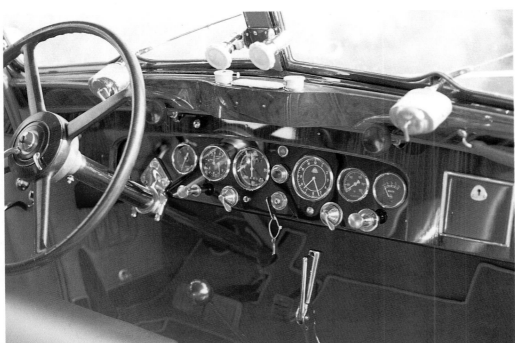

LEFT & OVERLEAF The Maybach Zeppelin Cabriolet Sport (*overleaf*) was comprehensively equipped. The photographs of the interior on this page show the high standards of finish attained by the Swabian coachbuilder Hermann Spohn who, after the war, worked with Mercedes and the sports-car manufacturer Veritas. The Spohn company ceased building car bodies in the late 1950s; the factory now houses a toy-making business

MERCEDES 60

BOTH PAGES With the same 9326 cc engine capacity as the 60 hp Mercedes, but with side valves instead of an F-head power unit, the 70 hp Mercedes was introduced in 1904. Some engines of this type were shipped to America where they were used in the American Mercedes assembled on Long Island. This actual 70 hp, after an adventurous career in Europe and South America, was discovered on a mission station in Argentina and brought back to England for restoration. It is now a star exhibit in the Filching Manor Motor Museum, near Eastbourne, Sussex

Just think: when the 60 hp Mercedes was launched in 1903, the overall speed limit in Britain was just 12 mph. The new Mercedes could attain seven times that velocity. The car industry, a helpless infant just seven years earlier, when its primitive horseless carriages could only legally move at walking pace, had rocketed to its first maturity with breathtaking speed. It's as though a manufacturer were to bring out a car today that a skilled driver could safely handle on the public roads at almost 500 mph.

Although the Mercedes could go racing and defeat the best that the world had to offer, it was originally created as a road car without equal, at the behest of the flamboyant Emil Jellinek, Austrian Consul-General in Nice and unofficial agent for the German Daimler company.

Jellinek indulged his passion for speed at the wheel of the most powerful cars he could persuade the Daimler company to build for him, and thereby entranced his rich friends into buying replicas of these ungainly brutes; the 24 hp Daimler of 1899 was an elephantine device whose

great height and short wheelbase were an infallible recipe for unpredictable handling. Wishing for something better, faster, safer, Jellinek commissioned Daimler's brilliant designer Wilhelm Maybach to create 'the car of the day after tomorrow'.

Reactionary old Gottlieb Daimler, who had founded his company in the 1880s to manufacture internal combustion engines, built his first powered carriage in 1896 and, wishing for nothing more adventurous, died in March 1900. Less than a month later Jellinek signed a contract worth half a million marks for the first batch of thirty cars of the new design; they were to be called Mercedes, the name of his teenage daughter, to lessen sales resistance in France, where memories of the Franco-Prussian War of 1870 were still bitter. The Daimler

The magnificent Mercedes motor car, manifestly, is not the carriage for the man of moderate means, but rather for the modest millionaire. . . . The beauty, elegance and symmetry of her form are beyond question. Although endowed with a fleetness which is terrifying when she is asked to do her best, although capable of tearing up roof-like hills at a speed which, if accomplished on the flat by an express train would, by many railway directors, be called excessive, yet this dear creature at the touch of her master's — nay, let us say, lover's — hand on the throttle control, will gently crawl along behind a four-wheeled cab as smoothly and quietly as a phantom. But when the road is clear and her lover sees no reason why she should not be indulged, the throttle is gently opened, and, with unparalleled rapidity of acceleration, the speed increases, the wind is split in twain by her fair form and rushed by the driver's ears, and when the inexperienced passenger thinks the utmost possible pace has been reached, the fourth speed is suddenly slipped in, she bounds forward and is skimming the road surface at nearly 80 miles an hour.

The Magnificent Mercedes, by Claude Johnson, 1904

Early cars like this Mercedes had huge sprockets (*top picture*) to transmit their immense power to the rear wheels by chain. Neither driver nor riding mechanic could help but be aware of the gnashing of metal at high speed in close proximity to the open cockpit!

company quickly adopted the Mercedes name for all their cars, the two accents persisting until the merger with Benz took place in 1926.

The Mercedes car was the epitome of advanced design – for the first time it combined a pressed-steel chassis, equal-sized wheels, gate gearchange, honeycomb radiator mounted ahead of

the engine and mechanically operated inlet valves – but it was unproven. That hasty development was all too obvious at the debut of the new Mercedes at the February 1901 Grand Prix de Pau. 'It was so untuned that it was quite impossible to more than guess at its capabilities', reported a keen observer of the early racing scene, Gerald Rose.

The guessing was over just a few short weeks later: the new Mercedes cars swept the board at the Nice Autocar meeting and Werner's example was the fastest petrol car present, covering the flying kilometre in 41.8 sec (53.5 mph). The Werner car also won the Nice-Salon-Nice race at an average speed of 36 mph and was fastest car up the La Turbie hillclimb.

From that moment, the Mercedes was 'the car that set the fashion to the world'. Wealthy sportsmen were so keen to own Mercedes cars that in March 1903 Daimler could announce that it had sold the whole of its production of Mercedes to English customers for months ahead. The reason was almost certainly the introduction of the new 60 hp Mercedes, a blindingly fast machine with a 9236 cc four-cylinder engine, an exclusive and exceedingly dangerous toy for well heeled private owners – it cost some £1800 in chassis form, and could incur a tyre bill of £500 a year.

The perils of Mercedes 60 ownership were quickly brought home by a fatal accident to the popular sportsman Count Eliot Zborowski at La Turbie. 'The Count was driving one of the new 60 hp Mercedes, and is said to have been very nervous at starting', telegraphed a correspondent to the weekly magazine *The Autocar.* 'He had had little or no time to have become accustomed to his car.' It appeared that Zborowski had caught the hand throttle lever on the steering wheel with his elegantly starched shirt cuffs and jammed it open. . . .

Control of those first 60s was ingenious, if lacking a certain amount of delicacy: the hand throttle pulled and pushed on the end of a long toothed rack which rotated coarse-threaded collars to vary the lift of the valves and thus the amount of mixture inhaled by the huge cast-iron pistons at every revolution. Low-tension ignition relied on an extra set of tappets which separated within the cylinder to cause a spark.

This was truly the first sports car – and the Daimler works expected even greater things of the 90 hp racers which it had entered for the premier racing event of 1903, the Gordon Bennett Trophy. The 90 hp Mercedes never had an adequate chance to prove itself, however; in June, fire reduced the wood-framed Daimler works and seventy Mercedes cars to ashes, including all the 90 hp racers. The twisted remains of one of these, which had cost £3500 to build, were sold for £60.

The loyalty of private owners to the Mercedes marque was remarkable,

BELOW A riding mechanic was essential in the days when the supply of oil to the engine was controlled by a battery of drip-feed lubricators mounted on the dashboard

though: enough of them lent their 60s to the works to enable Mercedes to field a full team in the race (held on a figure-of-eight course in Ireland because racing was banned in England). It was the Mercedes 60 of the rich American Clarence Gray Dinsmore that won the Gordon Bennett, driven by the 'Red Devil' – Belgian ace Camille Jenatzy. That was the amazing achievement of the Mercedes 60 – a road-going car, unmodified save for the replacement of its touring bodywork, yet

capable of winning the world's premier international motor race.

Just a handful of Mercedes of the pre-1905 era survive and to drive one of the big sporting models is a rare privilege. The unique 1904 Mercedes 70 hp two-seater owned by Paul Foulkes-Halbard has, like the 60s, an engine displacing 9236 cc, though with a T-head configuration rather than the F-head layout of the 60; its adventurous life included a spell as a railcar in the mountains of Argentina, where it was discovered in the 1960s.

The official stamp of the Automobile Club de France on a dumb-iron indicates a possible racing career in the days when giant racers thundered from city to city across the dusty roads of Europe, but the mystery may never be resolved. What *is* certain is that this Mercedes 70 is a car that loves to be driven hard. A magnificent performer, and still capable of some 85 mph, it is unforgiving of driver error. Yet with that massive engine pounding away insistently – at top speed, it's only turning at some 1200 rpm, so high is the gearing – and the direct, responsive steering, that the Mercedes makes you feel like a primitive god at the wheel.

BOTH PAGES & OVERLEAF In its heyday, a car like this Mercedes 70hp would have had a variety of bodies in the motor house for racing and touring; today, the car wears lightweight aluminium racing seats built by Carrosserie Rothschild, pioneers of all-metal construction in the early years of the century (*left and overleaf*). Its owner, Paul Foulkes-Halbard, recalls that his Mercedes featured in a classic motor book, *En Route*, published in 1908, as 'the finest touring car in existence'

MERCEDES-BENZ SS

I love you, my heavenly wonder express,
My rushingest, buzzingest, hummingest, S!
Kurt Juhn, *Danke S*, 1929

It was to give the aviators of Imperial Germany the ability to fly higher than their Allied rivals that Mercedes began experimenting with forced induction in 1915; two types of supercharged aero-engine were produced, but this work was ended by the defeat of Germany in 1918. Nevertheless, Mercedes switched its attention to experiments with supercharged motor car engines, first attempts being concerned with the 10/30 hp Mercedes-Knight sleeve-valve power unit. The sleeves of that engine burned around the ports, so the engineers quickly turned their attention to the more robust poppet-valve engines.

Mercedes regarded the blower as a means of boosting engine power only when the driver called for it; thus a multiple-disc clutch, operated by 'clean-cut pressure' on the accelerator pedal, was used to engage a train of gears turning the Roots-type supercharger at three or four times crankshaft speed to force air into the carburettor. The extravagant nature of this process was advertised by the buzz-saw scream of the power unit when the blower was engaged; nevertheless, all the blown Mercedes of the 1920s and 1930s used this system of supercharging. If Paul Daimler, son of the company's founder, had started the ball rolling, it was his successor as chief designer, Ferdinand Porsche, who really made the words 'supercharger' and 'Mercedes'

synonymous in the latter part of the 1920s.

Porsche's first supercharged sports Mercedes were the type 400 4-litre and the type 630 6-litre. The latter car was better known as the 24/100/140, the three figures representing its taxable, unblown and blown horsepower ratings. Porsche's light-alloy, dual-ignition, overhead-camshaft engine was built in

unit with a four-speed gearbox, and the 24/100/140 promised much; but when the model went on sale in 1924, it quickly became clear that although Porsche was skilful at designing engines, he was not such a clever chassis engineer, for the car's performance was way ahead of its handling. . . .

The first step towards rectifying this fairly basic shortcoming was made when

BOTH PAGES This Mercedes-Benz 38/250SS won its class in the 1930 Ulster Tourist Trophy, driven by Malcolm Campbell. A similar car won the 1929 Ulster TT, run in pouring rain, driven by Rudolf Caracciola, nicknamed 'Der Regenmeister' (the Rain-master) — he drove the big car on the limit, supercharger screaming, to victory in the event

BOTH PAGES Malcolm Campbell entered the entire three-car Mercedes team in both the 1930 Ulster sports-car Grand Prix and the TT, with himself, Earl Howe and Rudolf Caracciola as drivers. Caracciola won the Grand Prix after a thrilling battle with Birkin's Blower Bentley, with Howe third and Campbell fifth on the road (as the Irish Grand Prix was a two-day handicap, they were placed fourth and sixth – but Mercedes still won the team prize)

the cantilever rear springs were replaced by semi-elliptics. Then Porsche redesigned the car on a shorter wheelbase to create the type K, for *Kurz* (short), first of the great supercharged Mercedes-Benz sports cars of the 1920s, and a car which numbered among its distinguished clientele that enigmatic monarch King Zog of Albania. That 6.25-litre 24/110/160 type K, claimed to be the world's first genuine 100 mph touring car, was still endowed with unforgiving handling, however, which earned it the nickname 'Death Trap'.

Mercedes merged with its old rival Benz in June 1926, and one of the first fruits of the union was the S series, derived from the earlier type K. For the S series, launched in February 1927, Porsche dramatically revised the design, lowering the chassis, enlarging the engine to 6.8 litres, fitting two carburettors instead of one and increasing the supercharger boost. It was a simple formula, but it worked: the lowered chassis improved the handling and the Mercedes-Benz type S quickly made a name for itself in the annals of motor sport. The larger-than-life Otto Merz, sometime chauffeur to the Archduke Franz Ferdinand of Austria and reputed to be able to drive six-inch nails into a plank with his bare hands, won the first

German Grand Prix at the newly opened Nürburgring in July 1927 at the wheel of a type S Mercedes: a similar car, driven by Christian Werner, made the fastest lap, averaging over 66 mph round the twisting circuit.

The type S was built very much for prestige; the firms's less glamorous lines – commercial vehicles and side-valve touring cars – were what made the money. Production of the S was, consequently, modest – Germany was in the limbo between the hyperinflation of the Weimar Republic and the Great Depression – and in 1927 just eighty type Ss were built, while in 1928 seventy-five left the factory. The S was officially catalogued for four years, but the bulk of production took place in those two years, the total output being only 164 cars.

RIGHT ABOVE & BELOW The 1930 Tourist Trophy type 38/250SS carries twin rear tyres. The 1929 winner Caracciola was disqualified before the 1930 Ulster TT because his car was fitted with the so-called 'elephant' blower, which had fourteen fins instead of the standard ten on the supercharger fitted to Campbell and Howe's cars (*below*). This was unfortunate, because it rained heavily during the race, ideal conditions for Caracciola

Alongside the S, late in 1928, Mercedes introduced a new model, the SS. In those relatively innocent pre-Hitler days, the initials stood for nothing more sinister than Super Sports and 102 such cars were built in 1928–9; the potential of the model was shown when 'Scrap' Thistlethwayte made the fastest lap (74.39 mph) in the 1928 Ulster Tourist Trophy. Thistlethwayte also made fastest lap (83.8 mph) in the 1929 Irish Grand Prix before retiring with a blown gasket.

The driver whose reputation was really made by the type S Mercedes was Rudy Caracciola, who gained a matchless reputation for driving the tricky supercharged cars in the rain. His nickname of 'Der Regenmeister' dated from his impressive victory in the 1926 German Grand Prix at the fast Berlin AVUS circuit on a dangerously slippery track surface. Driving a Mercedes SS, Caracciola won the 1929 Tourist Trophy race and defeated a team of three

4.5-litre 'Blower' Bentleys; the winning car was subsequently acquired by Earl Howe, who made fastest lap in the 1930 Ulster TT with it.

Although the SS Mercedes handled well, some cars suffered from chassis whip, to the extent that the fan blades could hit the radiator core; Caracciola's 1929 Ulster TT car had aircraft-type wire bracing to avoid this!

All the SS Mercedes were built in 1928–9, but most were sold in 1930–1 and the model was catalogued until 1934. Even rarer was the SSK, a short-chassis variant with a slightly larger blower, tailored for success in hillclimbing events; eleven SSKs were manufactured in 1928, twenty-five in 1929 and just one in 1931. There was also a liberally drilled derivative with a larger 'elephant' blower; the SSKL, L for *Leicht* (Light), was built as a works competition car, although a few were said to have been sold to very special order from 1930 on.

ABOVE The cockpit of the SS is dominated by the large steering wheel, necessary to effect the effort required to guide the huge car at high speed. Note how narrow is the driving compartment

The *annus mirabilis* of the SSKL was 1931. In that year, Caracciola won every event he entered with his SSKL – seven hillclimbs, the Eifelrennen and the German Grand Prix at the Nürburgring, the AVUS-Rennen at Berlin and the Mille Miglia road race. It was an outstanding performance by any standards and proved that the SSKL's handling was not as potentially lethal as history would have us believe.

The ultimate SSKL in terms of performance was the 'Zeppelin on wheels', a streamlined cigar-shaped racer, designed by the aerodynamicist Baron Reinhard von König-Fachsenfeld, which in

Construction of the 38/250SS Mercedes is robust to say the least yet when, during the 1929 TT, the Mercedes driven by strong-man Otto Merz was impeded by a damaged mudguard, Merz ripped it off at the roadside with his bare hands and continued the race

1932 won the 183-mile race at the Berlin AVUS with the aristocratic Manfred von Brauchitsch at the wheel. This last-ditch effort for the SSKL was a private venture; Caracciola was driving for Alfa Romeo in that year. With a top speed of more than 150 mph, the streamlined SSKL had the 200 000 crowd on its feet cheering as, after a thrilling duel that had lasted almost from the start, the Mercedes pulled away from Caracciola's Alfa on the final half-lap of the race to romp home at a sensational average speed of almost 121 mph. The combination of brute force and science had once again proved to be unbeatable for the German team.

MERCEDES-BENZ 540K

The perfectly proportioned sports roadster bodywork of this 1937 Mercedes-Benz 540K was built by Mercedes' own coachbuilding division at Sindelfingen. Just eleven 'special roadsters' were produced, although other leading German coachbuilders such as Erdmann & Rossi built similar bodies on the supercharged chassis

Curiously, it was Mercedes' first venture into the economy class, in 1931 with the type 170, that laid the foundation for the classic supercharged cars of the decade, for this popular 1692 cc six featured Mercedes's first all-round independent suspension system, with parallel transverse leaf springs at the front and swing axles at the rear. The experience gained at the lower end of the market encouraged Mercedes to fit independent suspension to their exclusive sports cars, so when the straight-eight 3796 cc 15/90/120 type 380 appeared in 1932 it was the first supercharged Mercedes to have independent suspension; the swing axles were retained at the rear, but the front suspension was by a pioneering (and widely copied) system of parallel wishbones with coil springs.

Designed for the new *Autobahnen* which were being built across Germany, the 380 had a four-speed gearbox with overdrive fourth gear for effortless high-speed cruising. Of typically massive construction, the 380 was offered with a range of attractive bodies – saloon, tourer, sports-roadster and three types of cabriolet – built by Daimler's own coachbuilding facility at Sindelfingen, a factory 9 miles south of the Mercedes works at Stuttgart, which had been built in 1917 to manufacture aero-engines for the Kaiser's air force. Turned into a body works after the Armistice, Sindelfingen built bodies for buses and trucks as well as cars, but despite its industrialised nature it retained a sense of line and proportion which was especially evident on the short-chassis 380K sports car.

There was not the same concern for

This is a master car, for the very few. The sheer insolence of its great power affords an experience on its own.
The Autocar, 1936

BOTH PAGES This is one of only 145 Mercedes 540Ks built during 1937; the car was very much an exclusive production for the highest in German society, and was regarded as the country's premier car, capable of a top speed in the region of 105 mph fully laden

mass, however: even in its rare two-seat roadster form – only seven of these were built – the 380K scaled 2 tons, and its 120 bhp power unit didn't exactly give sparkling performance (as a comparison, the contemporary Alfa 8C 2300 developed slightly more power from an engine two-thirds the size and only weighed half as much). So the Stuttgart designers took the easy way out and increased the engine size; the 380 – of which just sixty were built – was replaced by the 5018 cc type 500 in 1933.

The supercharged 100/160 bhp 500K was, claimed its makers, 'intended in every way to be a touring car, a very fast touring car', and with the blower engaged and the engine at its peak 3400 rpm the 500K could just edge past 100 mph in overdrive top. The blower was only there for momentary use, however – more than 10 seconds with the supercharger clutched in was courting mechanical disaster – and the advice was to run up to whatever cruising speed was desired and then, even at an effortless 80 mph, use the supercharger just to correct the speed if traffic slowed the Mercedes. Besides, the sound of the blower was an eldritch wail, like a buzzsaw cutting into a

baulk of timber, and would have in itself been insupportable for more than a few seconds at a time.

For those few seconds, the great car was transformed: 'One's foot goes hard down, and an almost demoniacal howl comes in . . . the rev counter and speedometer needles leap round their dials: there is perhaps no other car noise in the world so distinctive as that produced by the Mercedes supercharger', wrote H.S. Linfield of *The Autocar* in 1936.

That tremendous performance potential was the reason why top racing driver Goffredo 'Freddy' Zehender was retained as technical adviser and demonstration driver of the K cars by British Mercedes-Benz, since the supercharged Mercedes was one of the few genuine 100 mph road cars on the British market in the 1930s. However, there was still room for improvement, for the 500K weighed nearly 2½ tons empty. So, after 354 500Ks had been built, the model was replaced by the archetypal blown Mercedes of the 1930s, the 540K, in late 1936. This had an engine rated at 115/180 bhp and although a de Dion rear suspension was originally proposed lack of development time forced the retention

ABOVE The 5.4-litre power unit of the 540K Mercedes with the massive chromed external exhaust pipes that typify the arrogance of 1930s Germany

of the old swing-axle layout. The 540K was one of the first models developed under Mercedes' new chief engineer, ex-racing driver Max Sailer, who had succeeded Hans Nibel after Nibel's untimely death at the age of fifty-four in November 1934.

Although their flowing lines and external exhaust systems were the epitome of the *Sturm und Drang* of Nazi years, the 500/540 Mercedes range never made any impression on national or international competition – apart from an

unsuccessful entry in the Monte Carlo Rally by Jack Waters (better known as actor Jack Warner) and entries in the obligatory German reliability runs – a surprising fact since Mercedes was dominating Grand Prix racing at the same time. Nonetheless, the arrogance of their appearance and their manner of going endeared these supercharged Mercedes to the upper echelons of the Nazi Party, like the portly Herman Goering, who drove a 500K, and the unsmiling *Korpsfuhrer* Huhnlein, head of the Nazi state motorsport body, the NSKK – whose backing enabled the Mercedes and Auto Union racing cars to dominate the major races of the 1934–9 era – who annexed the 200 bhp 5.8-litre 580K shown at the 1939 Berlin Show for his personal use. Its claimed top speed of 140 mph would have made it the fastest production car of the 1930s, but the 580K never passed the prototype stage .... Just twelve were built in the period 1939–40, and all bar the show car were retained 'for experimental work'.

The manufacturing record of the 540K indicated the exclusive nature of the beast; in 1936 output was just ninety-seven, in 1937 Mercedes built 145, in 1938 the total was ninety-five and sixty-nine were produced in 1939 before the war brought production to a virtual end (three more were built up to July 1942). In contrast, Stuttgart turned out 90 000 of the popular 170V model in the period 1936–42....

In May 1938, Linfield tested a 540K for *The Autocar* and achieved the highest maximum speed achieved by any road test car up to that date: with three up, the car reached 104.65 mph on the track at Brooklands. The 540K had a four-speed gearbox, but top gear was now direct, rather than the overdrive ratio used on the 500K.

Late in 1938, a revised 540K made its appearance, with oval-section chassis tubes instead of the pressed-channel frame members; the valves followed racing practice in being sodium cooled.

At the beginning of 1939, a five-speed transmission with overdrive top was adopted; Mercedes optimistically claimed that 'even at full speed the running of the engine is now practically inaudible'.

To meet the demands of the *Autobahn* era, Mercedes produced a limited edition two-seat coupé on the 540K chassis: just six of these streamlined *Autobahn-Kuriers* were built. Nearly as rare was the flamboyant special roadster bodywork, for factory records indicate that only

eleven of this model were built on both the 500K and 540K chassis.

The desirability of this model was proved in 1988, when British antique dealer John Price discovered a 1936 500K special tourer in a Midlands lock-up garage where it had been lying since 1956, when its butcher owner had lost interest in it. Price bought the car from Arthur Dawson for £150 000 and entered it for Christie's summer auction sale at Beaulieu, where the experts predicted it might possibly fetch £500 000.

Its condition was unremarkable – mice had gnawed the upholstery and the damp conditions in the garage had contributed to the generally down-at-heel appearance of the car. Bidding was nevertheless keen

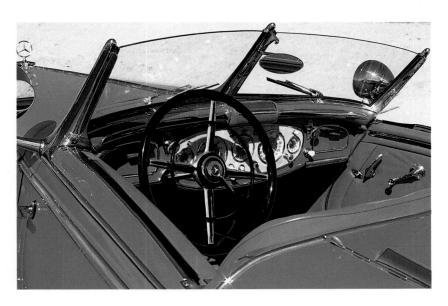

– and the car was quickly knocked down to the representative of Swedish businessman Hans Thulin for a record £1.6 million. The butcher, reported Christie's, 'was understood to be philosophical...'.

Mercedes planned to replace the 540K not with the 580K, but with an even more spectacular model, the 600K, which had a 6.0-litre V12 engine. A total of twenty-three 600Ks is believed to have been built between 1938 and 1942, but none seems to have survived.

ABOVE & OVERLEAF The luxurious nature of the 540K Roadster is shown in the well appointed cockpit; this is very obviously a fast tourer rather than a thinly disguised competition car. The swooping lines of the two-seater body (*overleaf*) belie the fact that this car scales over 2.5 tons

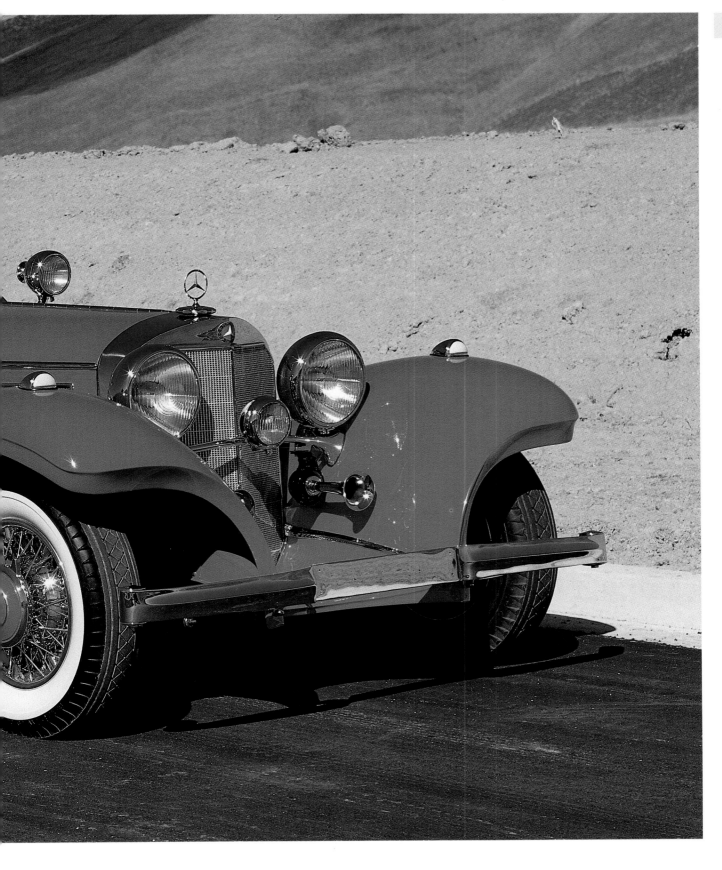

MERCER

They called the Mercer 'America's finest sports car', and the 'Car of Calibre'; this lithe and lovely two-seater was a motor car reduced to the bare minimum – bonnet, tiny scuttle cowl, two small bucket seats, fuel tank, little bustle tail beneath the spare tyres – and gloriously flowing wings. Yet this stark sportster was one of the most aesthetically satisfying cars ever built, *because* there was no surplus equipment. Seldom has a car advertised so plainly its purpose in life; but don't confuse its minimalist make-up with frailty. That car was designed to withstand far greater stresses than any normal driver could impose on it.

That's hardly surprising, because the financial backing that gave birth to the Mercer was provided by the Roebling family, the wealthy builders of Brooklyn Bridge, who, before the Mercer, had sponsored a little-known sportster called the Roebling-Planche, built from 1906 to 1909 and designed by a gifted Frenchman named Etienne Planche. Then, in 1910, they launched the Mercer, named for Mercer County, New Jersey, in which its Trenton factory was located.

C.G. Roebling, patriarch of the family, imbued the engineering team with his credo of 'surplus dimensions and extra quality in every single component', while his son, Washington Roebling II, was more interested in the performance of the cars. At first, Mercers were powered by proprietary T-head Beaver engines; among the prosaic tourers, a hint of the excitement to come was given by the Model 30-C Speedster, a canary-coloured runabout of rakish mien. Priced at just $1950, the Speedster could cruise at 60 mph – and, if the roads of the day could have supported it, keep up that gait for 500 miles, thanks to a fuel tank that held 40 gallons.

In 1910, young Washington Roebling II competed at the Wheatley Hills Course on Long Island in a stripped Mercer, a go-faster short-wheelbase version of the

Speedster known as the Type 30-M Raceabout: during 1911, the company's Chief Engineer, Finlay Robertson Porter, produced a road-going adaption of the racer, the Type 35-R Raceabout, intended to be 'safely and consistently' driven at over 70 mph. The 4926 cc 35-R, built on a 108 in wheelbase, was produced alongside more prosaic touring Mercers, like the M and O; these, it seemed, were more favoured by Porter,

Winning first and second in the light car race at Elgin was like taking candy from a baby; but to land third overall for the stock car championship was some achievement. One Mercer started and finished. One Lozier started and did not finish. Two Nationals started and only one finished. One Pope-Hartford started and did not finish. And of the three Alcos that started, one did not finish, and another was outrun by the Mercer.

Advertisement for Mercer car, 1911

BOTH PAGES Progenitor of the Type 35 Raceabout was the Beaver-engined Mercer 30-C Speedster of 1910, capable of sustaining a 60 mph cruising speed

for they had larger engines (5211 cc) and four speeds against the Raceabout's three. And when the M and O gained electric lighting and starting, for the 1914 season, the Raceabout still had Prestolite acetylene lamps and a crank-start; however, it had gained a fourth speed.

The first Raceabouts had single magneto ignition, developed around 60 bhp at a leisurely 2000 rpm and were guaranteed to cover a mile in 51 seconds – a speed of over 70 mph. Dual magneto

ignition was introduced on the Type 35-C, which scaled 1040 kg; the virtually identical 35-J, most famous of the Raceabouts, was slightly heavier at 1120 kg.

All the Mercer Raceabouts had forty-four-plate steel-to-steel clutches running

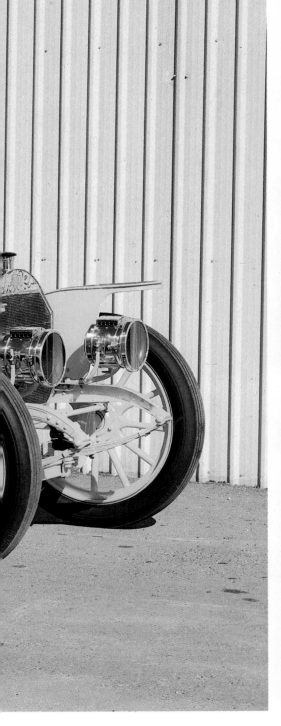

in oil for smooth power takeup, an engine mounted on a separate sub-frame and long springs of chrome-vanadium steel. Roadholding, even at the Mercer's normal 75 mph top speed, was outstanding while racing Type 35-J Mercers could attain 95 mph or more. An exciting touch was the 'outdoor' mounting of the throttle pedal, which stuck out beyond the shelter of the scuttle cowl so that a blast of high-speed air was forced up the right leg of the driver – but then, in those days, a standard joke was: 'How can you tell a happy motorist? – Easy, by the bugs stuck in his teeth.' However, some Raceabout owners fitted circular monocle windshields, carried on a hinged mounting clamped to the steering column.

The insistence on quality was paramount throughout the production process of the Raceabout; every chassis – and the firm never built more than 150 Raceabouts in a single year – was road-tested for several hundred miles before it was judged fit to be delivered to the fortunate owner.

While any colour was available to order, and a choice of three standard colours was given – red, brown or yellow – most owners chose that distinctive canary yellow that seemed so right for the Raceabout. Although the 35-J Raceabout remained in production until 1915, some of the fire went out of it in 1912, when Washington Roebling II went down with the *Titanic*.

Finlay Robertson Porter – who lived to see his Mercer Raceabout become one of the most highly sought-after American cars – resigned from Mercer in 1914 to build the FRP, a vee-radiatored 170 bhp luxury car, of which only a few examples were ever produced. He was succeeded as Chief Engineer by Erik H. Delling, who designed a new Raceabout, the 22/70, with a four-cylinder 80 bhp F-head engine of 4886 cc, to succeed the 35-J. Hardly in the stark tradition of its predecessor, the 22/70 Raceabout had such 'refinements' as a body with sides and a windscreen,

left-hand drive, central gearshift and an optional hood. As it was more 'civilised' than the original Raceabout, so the 22/70 was accordingly less desirable.

When in 1918, Mercer became part of the Hare's Motors Group (along with Locomobile and Crane-Simplex), Delling was replaced by A.C. Schultz, who designed the Series 4 and 5 Sportsters which even had electric starters, and a development of this, with a proprietary 5.5-litre Rochester ohv engine, was the sole product in the two years before Mercer finally ceased production in 1925. An attempt to revive the marque in 1931 saw only the building of two prototypes with Continental straight-eight engines.

BOTH PAGES Elegant detailing of the Mercer 30-C Speedster which, in comparison with the stark Raceabout it sired, was positively sybaritic. For instance, on the 30-C a streamlined cowl protected the driver's nether regions; on the Type 35-J, the throttle pedal was mounted in the full blast of the sidestream

With its 40-gallon fuel tank, the Mercer Type 30-C Speedster had a range of some 500 miles; modestly priced at $1950, the Speedster paved the way for the great days of the Mercer company

PACKARD V12

We believe the verdict of your friends will make you eager to drive one of the new Packards. Simply phone your Packard dealer and he will be glad to bring a car to your home. Drive it over a road you know by heart — test it in every way. Compare it on any basis you wish with any other fine cars, either American or foreign. And notice, too, that this newest and finest of all Packards has the lines that have made Packard America's most distinctive motor car — lines that make Packard one car the whole world recognises.

Packard advertisement, 1934

Packard were the first manufacturers in the world to put a V12-engined car into quantity production, their inspiration for this being a V12 racing car built for the Brooklands circuit by Sunbeam in 1913 and shipped across the Atlantic at the outbreak of war in Europe. Packard reacted with real haste, their gifted chief engineer, Jesse G. Vincent, having a V12 in the catalogue by May 1915: that first Twin-Six established Packard as the pace-setter among makers of luxury cars. It

also inspired a young Italian soldier named Enzo Ferrari to dream of building a V12-engined car....

It was to counter the launch of the 1930 V16 Cadillac that Packard retaliated with a new Twin-Six, however; this was developed in just 11 months, after plans to build a front-wheel-drive luxury car failed to pass the prototype stage. The coming of the new Packard was pure theatre: on the day of its announcement, 17 June 1931, the tickertape of the New

ABOVE & LEFT The radiator mascot of the Packard company, often referred to as a 'cormorant', actually depicts the legend of the pelican taking blood from its breast to feed its young. The 'pelican in her piety' was the family crest of Samuel Packard, who arrived in America in 1638 aboard the ship *Diligent*. This pelican is carried on a 1937 Packard V12 coupé, which epitomises the American concept of a sports car — it has a locker for golf clubs in the tail

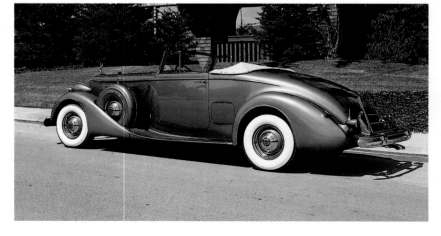

ABOVE & BELOW This 1937 Packard V12 is from the Fifteenth Series; one-fifth of all the Packard Twelves built during the 8 years of production were made in 1937 – but the days of custom coachwork were gone

York Stock Exchange traded tidings of doom and disaster for the news of the rebirth of the Packard Twin-Six. As Packard eschewed the tradition of the annual model change to coincide with each show season, choosing to bring out new 'Series' when they felt the time was right, the launch of the new Ninth Series Twin-Six generated maximum attention.

Its radical styling incorporated a vee-radiator whose shape was echoed in the headlamp shells and glasses and which carried a stylised mascot of a 'pelican in her piety', the family crest of Samuel Packard, who had arrived in America from England in 1638 aboard the ship *Diligent*. The car's massive bumpers had oil-damped spring-loaded harmonic stabilizers to absorb road shock. Vacuum-servo-assisted brakes and solenoid-engaged starter were other pointers to the future, although the brakes would remain mechanical until hydraulics came in with the Sixteenth Series of 1936.

The heart of the new-generation Twin-Six was a 7298 cc 67-degree V12 – a curious choice of angle – with aluminium cylinder heads, hydraulic valve silencers and thermostatically controlled twin downdraught carburettors with – another advanced touch – automatic chokes. Before it left Packard's Detroit factory, every Twin-Six engine had been turned over by an electric motor for an hour before it ran under its own power on the test bench for a further six hours. Finally, a

75-minute check-up on the dynamometer confirmed that it was developing the specified output of 160 bhp at 3200 rpm. Only then was the engine fitted in the chassis and taken to Packard's proving ground, opened in 1927 on a 500-acre site north of Detroit, to be given its final tune-up during a hundred fast laps of the 2.5-mile test track by racing driver Tommy Milton, who then signed the Packard's 'Certificate of Approval'.

Sadly, the new 1932 Twin-Six, available only with 'Individual Custom' bodywork by Dietrich, was overpriced at $6500–$6950 and a mere 549 of the 16 613 Ninth Series cars produced by Packard between 17 June 1931 and 7 January 1933 were V12-engined. So those Dietrich bodies built during the 1932 model year were still available on the V12 Packard chassis in 1934! Cheaper models were added to the catalogue in January 1932, at prices ranging from $3895 to $4195, but a mere six months later they were all increased in price by $500.

For the Tenth Series, announced on 5 January 1933, Packard dropped the name Twin-Six, which they thought might be inhibiting sales, in favour of the less romantic Twelve – and sold just 520 of them out of a Series total of 4800, between 5 January and 21 August 1933.

The Tenth Series Twelve was based on a new X-braced chassis frame, which set the pattern for Packards for two decades to come. A mighty performer – it could accelerate from 5 to 30 mph in top gear in just 8.5 seconds – the new Twelve rode on 17 in wheels (the Ninth Series had ridden on 18 in wheels) and boasted variable-servo power brakes controlled by a four-position selector on the dashboard.

During the short currency of the Tenth Series, a very special Packard Twelve carried off every automotive prize at the Chicago Century of Progress exhibition. The last design produced by Ray Dietrich at Dietrich Inc before he left the company

he had founded in 1927, this 'Car of the Dome' was a metallic-bronze sport sedan with chromed wire wheels. Its interior metal brightwork, from door handles to throttle pedal, was gold-plated, trim was in beige English broadcloth, and a sheared beaver rug lay in the rear compartment. All the wood trim was in burr Carpathian elm and the built-in bar (Prohibition had ended less than three months earlier!) was backed with a gold-mounted mirror and contained four golden goblets and two crystal glasses.

Crowds queued for up to two hours at the Travel and Transportation Building just to see the Car of the Dome, which, after the exhibition closed, toured the Packard dealerships. Some of its styling features found their way on to the Eleventh Series Twelve, launched on 21 August 1933, which also boasted a new lubrication system; this enabled a new Twelve to sustain a steady 112 mph at the Packard Proving Grounds for 56 hours before a big end failed and brought the run to a halt.

ABOVE The Packard V12 engine was one of the classic American power units: just 5774 Packard V12 cars were built and sold. Enthusiastic owners claimed that the 1937–9 Packard V12 was 'the nearest thing to steam' – it could accelerate from 3 to 30 mph in top gear in just 8.5 seconds

BOTH PAGES The classic Packard V12; this 1933 Tenth Series car carries custom coupé coachwork by Dietrich; a sister car, a Sport Sedan designed by Ray Dietrich, carried off every automotive prize at the 1933 Chicago World's Fair

The Eleventh Series combined elegance, luxury and advanced engineering to a remarkable degree, right down to a built-in radio, a combined speedometer/tachometer which indicated the engine speed in top gear and automatic reversing lights. Semi-custom bodies offered on the Eleventh Series Twelve were speedsters and sport phaetons by LeBaron, who also constructed three streamlined sport coupes for show purposes, previewing the styling of the forthcoming Twelfth Series, introduced on 30 August 1934.

However, the great days of the Packard V12 ended with the Eleventh Series – and even then sales totalled only 960 cars; the V12 model survived until 1939, when the Seventeenth Series Twelves – all 446 of them – were assembled against individual order only, from such celebrities as 'Yankee Doodle Dandy' George M. Cohan, King Gustav V

of Sweden and the White House. Franklin D. Roosevelt's last Twelve was a very special automobile, designed to resist the attack of an assassin, with body and windows armoured to withstand a direct hit from a 50-calibre machine gun bullet, and a folding hood specially reinforced to withstand a grenade dropped from a height of 250 feet.

By August 1939, the Packard Twelve was gone for good, after a production run of 5744 cars in eight years: but there was a distinguished coda to the story of the car, for 1938 had seen the start of production of a new twelve-cylinder Packard marine engine destined for the nation's wartime patrol boats, and, like Ford of Britain, Packard built more Rolls-Royce Merlin V12 aero-engines during the war than did Rolls-Royce. Perhaps, as the original Twin-Six had been inspired by a British V12 aero-engine, this wartime reciprocation was entirely appropriate.

The Depression saw the Pierce-Arrow company of Buffalo, New York, one of America's longest-established and most outstanding luxury-car manufacturers, in deep financial trouble: an ill-starred merger with Studebaker had done nothing for the exclusive image of Pierce-Arrow (founded in 1865, bizarrely, to make bird and squirrel cages), and sales had tumbled from seven thousand cars in 1930 to a mere 2692 in 1932, despite a new V12 model launched on 9 November 1931. The hard times brought no stinting on the specification of the V12 Pierce-Arrow, however: there were seventeen body styles, three model lines, two engine displacements – 6524 cc and 7035 cc – three wheelbases – 137 in, 142 in and 147 in – wire, wooden or steel road wheels, freewheel, ride control and one of the very first factory-fitted radio installations.

The 1933 Pierce-Arrows were available in forty-five different body styles, at prices from $2785 to $7200, and had redesigned power units of 7035 cc and 7566 cc with the first direct-acting hydraulic tappets to go into production in America. These engines were particularly smooth-running and reliable: in September 1932, a 7566 cc V12 roadster driven by 'Mormon Meteor' Ab Jenkins set an unofficial World 24-Hour Speed Record of 112.91 mph at the Bonneville Salt Flats in Utah.

A month later, Pierce-Arrow Vice-President Roy Faulkner commissioned twenty-five-year-old freelance designer Philip Ogden Wright – who had recently left the Art & Color Section of General Motors – to design 'the car built in the 1930s for the 1940s' as the centrepiece of Pierce-Arrow's exhibit at the 1933 Chicago Century of Progress exhibition, an expression of confidence in the future that perhaps marked the turning point at which America began to emerge from the depression.

It took just three months for Studebaker's body department, working

The micrometer, not the clock, governs the building of each Pierce-Arrow. The engine . . . goes through 350 skilled hands and nearly one hundred inexorable tests. Instruments as sensitive as seismographs attest the balance of many of its parts. Even when it is running with whisper silence on the dynamometer, Pierce-Arrow experts may dismantle and reconstruct to correct some microscopic irregularity. The clock means nothing, the micrometer everything.

Advertisement for the Pierce-Arrow V12, 1931

under engineer James Hughes, to build Wright's 'Silver Arrow', its avant-garde styling the result of wind-tunnel experiments.

Since 1912, Pierce-Arrow had been distinguished by headlamps mounted on the wings, rather than in the conventional position on the dumb-irons, but it was only with the creation of the Silver Arrow that this lamp location really looked a logical part of the styling. Indeed, the Silver Arrow, built on a 7566 cc Pierce V12 chassis, represented one of the first instances in which the car had been treated as an integral piece of rolling sculpture. The housings of those fender-mounted lamps, set either side of a gently-raked radiator shell, flowed smoothly into the rising belt line of the full-width passenger compartment.

RIGHT & BELOW Under its futuristic skin, the Silver Arrow was unashamedly a luxury car of the 1930s, with broadcloth upholstery and birdseye maple woodwork much in evidence

Two-tone paint – the bodywork painted silver with the relief panels around the windows and on the bonnet-top picked out in darker grey – accentuated the sleek lines of the car. The smooth contours of the tapering tail were interrupted only by a tiny 'eyebrow' window whose twin panes were elongated triangles. The twin spare wheels were concealed within the front wings, while the rear wheels were covered by pontoon wings.

If the exterior of the Silver Arrow looked fitted for the Flash Gordon future envisaged by the America of the 1930s, inside, the car was traditionally luxurious, with broadcloth upholstery and birdseye maple woodwork; rear compartment passengers were supplied with a radio set and duplicate instruments.

Wright's 'harmonious and impressive' Silver Arrow went as well as it looked, with a 115 mph top speed a clear tribute to its aerodynamic lines. Only that widow's peak of a rear window would have made the car stand out in a line-up of 1950s luxury vehicles. Even though all the automotive prizes at the Century of Progress exhibition went to a conservatively styled V12 Packard, the popular honours went to the Pierce-Arrow.

The Silver Arrow's impact on car design is hard to assess – certainly many of its design features were to be adopted by other manufacturers, but it brought little commercial success to its manufacturers. Pierce-Arrow built five identical Silver Arrows, priced at $10 000 each, and claimed that RKO film star Ginger Rogers – 'Radio's Terpsichore' – had bought one of them, although she was not yet at the peak on her fame as partner to Fred Astaire.

Five more, less radical, 'production' Silver Arrows followed in 1934, but they had little in common with Philip Wright's

BELOW The flowing rear aspect of the Silver Arrow incorporates this unique – and slightly sinister – rear-window treatment, which must have afforded only a minimal view of the world behind

Remarks design historian Strother McMinn: 'It is almost impossible today to imagine the Silver Arrow's shattering impact – it marked a radical change from the careful evolution of traditional design'. The full-width front wings of the Silver Arrow were not only aerodynamically efficient – they also housed the twin spare wheels

original concept except for the fastback body styling. Wright later joined Briggs Bodies, where he worked under another great body designer, Dutch-born John Tjaarda, creator of the original Lincoln-Zephyr, a design which had much in common with the Silver Arrow. In 1939 he joined Packard, later freelanced for Willys-Overland, and went on to work for Douglas Aircraft as a technical

illustrator. Philip Wright died in Long Beach, California, in 1982.

The critical acclaim achieved by the Silver Arrow marked a new departure for the car side of Pierce-Arrow, which a consortium of Buffalo businessmen bought from Studebaker – which had been placed under receivership – in August 1933. Against all odds, Pierce-Arrow recorded a profit in its first three

months under the new ownership; it was to be the company's last quarter in profit.

Although the cars were steadily improved, sales went in the opposite direction until the pride of Buffalo shuffled off its mortal coil in the spring of 1938: indeed, the 1938 Pierce-Arrows – only seventeen were produced – were assembled after the lines had stopped for the last time. Pierce-Arrow was declared insolvent in April 1938, and its assets, worth almost $1 million, were sold for a mere $40 000.

The Silver Arrow had briefly established Pierce-Arrow as the style-setter in the luxury car field, but the company had lacked the courage to build on that advantage. Today only those still-futuristic Silver Arrows testify to the glory that might have been....

At whatever speed this car is being driven on its direct third, there is no engine so far as sensation goes, nor are one's auditory senses troubled, driving or standing, by a fuller sound than emanates from an eight-day clock. There is no realisation of driving propulsion; the feeling as the passenger sits either at front or back of the vehicle is of being wafted through the landscape. We cannot refrain from describing the production of such an engine as this as a great triumph of engineering skill on the part of that engineering genius, Mr Royce.

The Autocar, 1907

Henry Royce was born in 1863 (the same year as Henry Ford), the son of a miller who fell on hard times. The Royce family was forced to move to London, where young Henry's father died in 1872 and the boy had to sell newspapers to supplement the meagre family income; their staple diet was bread and jam. Young Royce had only an intermittent education, but he was an intelligent lad and so impressed his aunt that she arranged for him to become an apprentice with the Great Northern Railway locomotive works in Peterborough. After three years, Royce's aunt could no longer afford to fund him, so he walked north seeking work and joined a tool-making company in Leeds, which paid 11 shillings (55 pence) for a 54-hour week.

In his spare time, Royce studied the new science of electricity, which enabled him to get a job with the Electric Light and Power Company in London. After a while, he pooled his savings of £20 with the £50 of a friend to create an electrical engineering business in Manchester: their first minor success was a cheap electric door-bell which sold at 1s 6d (batteries not included!). Royce then turned to the design and manufacture of a sparkless electric motor and in 1894 began the manufacture of electric cranes; by 1899 sales were running at £20 000 annually.

Royce's hard work put a severe strain on his health and he was advised to spend more time in the open air, so he took up the new sport of motoring, buying a second-hand 10 hp Decauville and trying to improve its design. This persuaded him to build three 10 hp Royce cars, inspired by the Decauville. One of these was bought by Henry Edmunds, who introduced his friend the Hon Charles Stewart Rolls to Royce.

Rolls, the wealthy third son of Lord Llangattock, had, in 1894, been the first Cambridge undergraduate to own a motor car, and he decided to put his social contacts to good commercial use by going into business as a motor dealer. To sell alongside the high-quality Continental cars for which he was an agent, he began looking for a suitable small car, and asked his friend Henry Edmunds to inform him of any promising small cars he might happen to come across.

Edmunds recommended an inspection of the new Royce car, and after a ride on it, Rolls boasted: 'I have met the greatest engineer in the world'. C.S. Rolls & Co were appointed sole agents for the marque and it was agreed that the cars would be known as Rolls-Royces.

After building cars with two, three, four, six and eight cylinders, Royce decided to concentrate on making an improved six-cylinder model, which he planned to be 'The Best Car in the World'. Its side-valve 7046 cc engine had its cylinders cast in two blocks of three and was rated at 40/50 hp. Typical of the care with which the car had been designed were the front engine mountings, which allowed the chassis frame to flex without stressing the power unit, but the wires and pipes which neatly festooned the exterior of the engine led one French magazine to caption a photograph of the Rolls-Royce power unit as 'under the brushwood'.

The 40/50 hp Rolls-Royce was to remain in production for nineteen years and even saw duty during World War I,

carrying weighty armour-plated bodywork, but the marque's enviable reputation for supreme quality was founded squarely on the achievements of the thirteenth 40/50 hp chassis to be constructed, which was christened the *Silver Ghost*.

The commercial genius of Rolls-Royce was Claude Johnson – sometimes called 'the hyphen in Rolls-Royce' – an ex-journalist and former secretary of the Automobile Club of Great Britain & Ireland. When Rolls was killed in an aeroplane accident at Bournemouth in 1910 and Royce's health broke down from overwork a year later, it was Johnson who kept the Rolls-Royce company afloat. While Royce still supervised design work, he never returned to the factory at Derby where

BOTH PAGES Determined to prove the supremacy of the new Rolls-Royce 40/50hp six-cylinder, the company's commercial genius, Claude Johnson, took the thirteenth chassis of the new series, had it fitted with a silver-painted body and silver-plated lamps, and christened it the *Silver Ghost*. He then put it through a 15 000-mile observed test and it cost just £2.13 to return it to as-new condition

RIGHT To modern eyes, the layout of the *Silver Ghost*'s engine seems neat enough, but in 1907 the French magazine *Omnia* captioned a photograph of this power unit 'under the brushwood' because of its external pipes and wires

the company had moved in 1907, but continued to operate from a succession of convalescent homes in England and France.

It was Johnson who in June 1907 entered the *Silver Ghost* for a 15 000-mile reliability test observed by the RAC. Although the Rolls-Royce wasn't the first car to undertake such a test – three months earlier, a 45 hp six-cylinder Hotchkiss had started on a similar trial – the performance of the Rolls-Royce was outstanding, for the *Silver Ghost* was not detained on the road by any mechanical problem; indeed, its only involuntary stop (apart from the inevitable punctures) occurred after 629 miles, when the petrol tap vibrated shut on an appallingly bad road surface.

During the test, the *Silver Ghost* spent 40 hr 13 min in the workshop for routine maintenance; the primitive state of the highways (and of tyres, which Rolls-Royce *didn't* make) was shown by the total of £187 12s 6d (£187.63) spent on tyres, at £12 0s 9d (£12.04) for a front tyre, £13 5s 9d (£13.29) for a rear. The total running

cost for the period, during which the *Silver Ghost* covered more than 300 miles every day, averaged less than 2p per mile and the few replacement parts deemed necessary to restore the car to as-new condition cost just £2 2s 7d (£2.13).

The Rolls-Royce was capable of accelerating from 4 to 53 mph in direct drive third speed and – under exceptional conditions – attaining a maximum of 63 mph in overdrive top; remarkably, its overall fuel consumption was 17.8 mpg. Thus proven as a reliable and economical form of luxury transport, the 40/50 hp Rolls-Royce went into full production at the rate of four chassis a week, the cars being known familiarly, if incorrectly, as Silver Ghosts. Before long, the overdrive top was discontinued because Edwardian motorists, misunderstanding its purpose, attempted to use it constantly instead of the direct-drive third ... and complained of the noise.

The hard-working *Silver Ghost* took Johnson on holiday to Cornwall in September 1907 and was sold during the following year to Dan Hanbury, one of the Rolls-Royce company's travelling inspectors. He covered some 500 000 miles in the next thirty-nine years, then in 1947 Rolls-Royce were asked if they could provide the necessary parts for a refit. However, Dan Hanbury died during that winter, so Rolls-Royce acquired the *Silver Ghost* and carried out the restoration themselves.

Since then, the old *Silver Ghost* has continued to work hard for its living and has probably covered another 100 000 miles in the hands of its makers. In 1982, it travelled from Glasgow to London, following a similar route to that used during the 15 000-mile RAC trial 75 years earlier and then left on a commemorative visit to the United States.

Shortly after its return, this writer was fortunate enough to travel in the passenger seat of the car; despite that astronomical mileage behind it, the *Silver Ghost* is still a refined and comfortable Edwardian motor car; and, driven with regard for that overdrive gearbox, it *is* quieter than its rivals.

How does the *Silver Ghost* compare with its contemporaries? Dennis Miller-Williams, who in the course of his years at Rolls-Royce drove the car further than anyone else during the forty years since it returned to its makers and took it all round the world on promotional trips, has the answer.

'Considering that this is a car designed in 1906 and first put on the road in 1907, its general feel is modern', he commented. 'It doesn't feel like a veteran at all and the only things which really date it are the very direct steering and the brakes, which are only on the rear wheels. So you have to leave braking distances which are more in tune with the conditions of the days when the car was new and drive with considerable care in modern traffic.

'It has a comfortable ride, with the huge slow-revving engine developing its maximum torque at only 1800 rpm.

'At low revs, the car is extremely comfortable and quiet. Having driven other cars of this period, I can appreciate the considerable qualities of this car, which, for a 1907 vehicle, is actually nicer to drive than some cars of the 1920s and 1930s.

'One is very aware of the great skill that has gone into putting the car together, but Royce's achievement lay in making it easy to comprehend. It has no hidden vices or tricks, although you have to be very careful on sharp turns. On full lock, the road wheels can actually take over and wrench the wheel from your hands – you needed very strong wrists. . . .

'The car is always a reliable starter, provided the carburettor is set correctly.

BELOW It was common practice in the days of leather-faced cone clutches to prop out the clutch when the car was not in use – as seen in the photograph of the pedals of the *Silver Ghost* – to prevent the lining from 'freezing' so that the clutch would not disengage. While other makers labelled their ignition controls 'advance' and 'retard', Henry Royce felt that this sounded too French and inscribed the ignition quadrants of his cars 'Early' and 'Late'

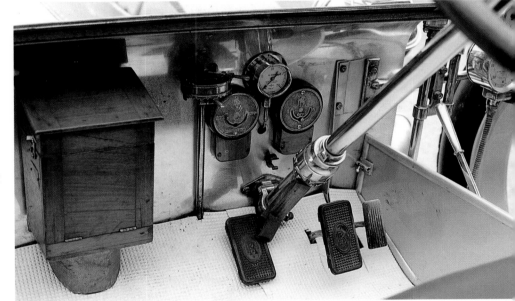

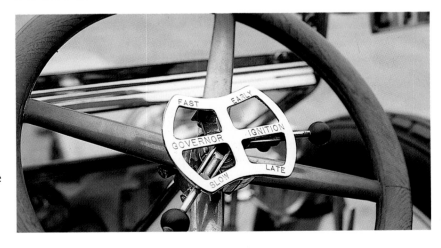

Although it has covered over half a million miles, the *Silver Ghost* bears its years lightly. It was this particular car above all which justified the Rolls-Royce claim that they built 'the best car in the world'

With the ignition fully retarded, you only have to pull up the starting handle from 9 o'clock to 12 o'clock, but if the spark is not set properly, it can throw you. In fact, it's not a difficult car to start at all, except in extremely cold weather, when the oil is less fluid.

'The leather-lined cone clutch has a large area and is easy to let in and out; consequently, you can take up the drive extremely smoothly. The early cars had a drip feed to keep the clutch lining moist.

'The technique is to get into direct drive and do considerable distances in that ratio. Of course, the *Ghost* has modest acceleration and a top speed of only 55 mph, but you have to remember that the speed limit then (and for many years after) was only 20 mph. These early cars have what Royce called a 'sprinting gear' – an overdrive fourth speed – and you normally drive in the direct ratio, which is third gear. Royce eventually dropped the sprinting gear because it *is* noisy. It doesn't take much of a slope to make you change down, and the overdrive is only really of much use on the level or going downhill.

'Having no top, the *Silver Ghost* has "total air conditioning" – the weather outside is the same as it is inside! Yet the car is capable of quite considerable feats, like the 15 000-mile trial and being driven in top gear from Scotland to London, which would have been easier on the roads of those days. I repeated the feat many years later on modern roads – even then, it was quite an achievement.' There are certainly few cars of this vintage which could have achieved feats such as these in their heyday, let alone over half a century later.

Was the *Silver Ghost* really a car without fault? Dennis Miller-Williams has reservations: 'If you polish all the silver-plated items properly, all the lamps, the nuts and bolts and other parts, it takes exactly six hours!' Even on such an exceptional car, the chauffeur's lot, it seems, was not a happy one.

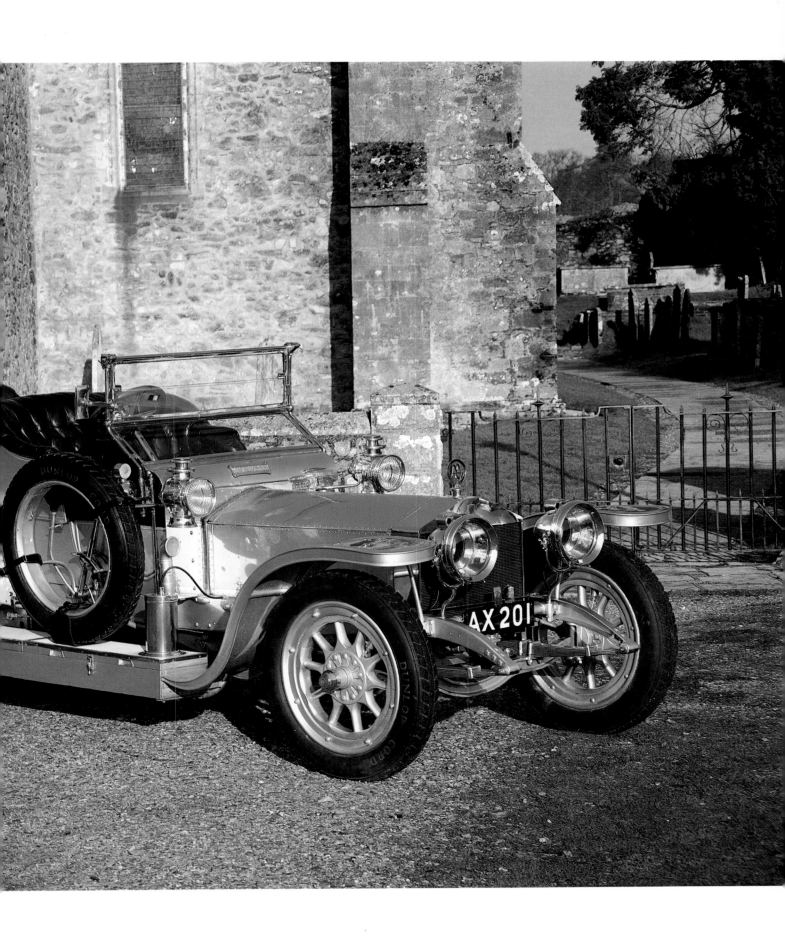

TALBOT-LAGO

One of the most convoluted car manufacturing combines of the 1920s was the Sunbeam-Talbot-Darracq group, which built cars in both England and France. When it collapsed in 1935, its English arm was snapped up by the Rootes brothers, former car agents, whose manufacturing group consisted entirely of companies which they had rescued from bankruptcy. Rootes had no interest in the French end of the organisation, which was snapped up by its works manager, an anglicized Italian called Major Antonio 'Tony' Lago. Known originally as Darracq, and sometimes as Talbot-Darracq, the Suresnes, Paris-based firm was refloated with backing from the French component industry and renamed Automobiles Talbot. No-one worried that the Talbot in question was the heraldic dog from the armorial bearings of an English nobleman, the Earl of Shrewsbury & Talbot, who had helped found the Clement Talbot company in Kensington at the turn of the century.

Lago's first task was to revitalise the flagging image of the company and the transformation of the French Grand Prix into a sports car event in the mid 1930s gave him the excuse he needed to produce a sports-racing derivative of the six-cylinder cars he had just launched.

His engineer, Walter Becchia, designed a new 4-litre engine derived from the old Talbot-Darracq 3-litre unit; its most ingenious feature was a cylinder head in which inclined valves in a hemispherical combustion chamber were actuated by crossover pushrods from a single camshaft, rather like the arrangement in the newly introduced BMW. In standard form, the new engine developed 165 bhp

and tuned for racing, with a 9.1:1 compression ratio, it was even more powerful, yet could run on the road on Discol pump fuel (alcohol was added to the fuel for track use).

The Talbot-Lago Speciale sports racer appeared during 1936, with similar bodywork to that of the contemporary Delahaye racers. Although the cars from Suresnes failed to win in their first season, third places in both the Marne and Comminges races and a record lap in the first Sports Car GP at Montlhéry revealed the potential of the new engine. 'Hoodless, screenless and bodied almost to the limit of frugality', the Talbot-Lago Special was designed as a racer, but also turned out to be a peerless road car.

The sensuous lines of this Talbot-Lago coupé by Figoni & Falaschi (nicknamed 'Phoney and Flashy' by English cynics) were described by William Lyons of Jaguar – no mean stylist himself – as 'positively indecent'

The machine has a wonderful stability; it is doubtful whether, except in a racing type of car, it would be possible to corner faster or more safely.
The Autocar, 1939

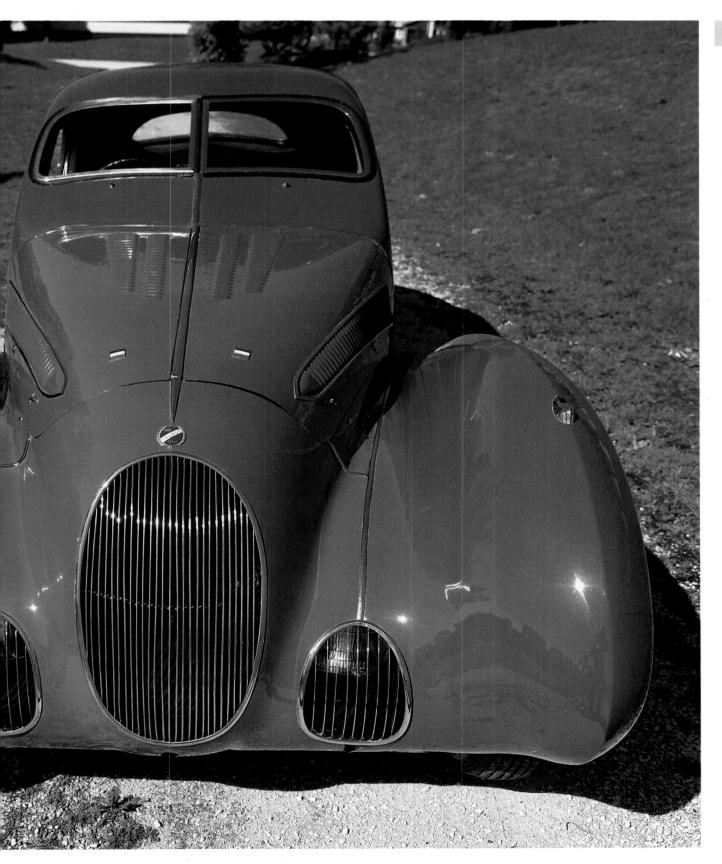

The works sports-racer, which was driven to victory in the 1937 ACF Sports Car GP at Montlhéry by Louis Chiron and in that year's Donington TT by Gianfranco Comotti, was sold to the British driver A.C. Lace, who drove it with Ian Connell in the 1938 TT finishing fifth. Connell bought the car from his co-driver and won many Brooklands events with it. He came a close second to Dobson's Delahaye 135 in the 'Fastest Road Car' race, when his Talbot-Lago was shown to have a top speed of 140 mph and was only once beaten in a sprint – and then by less than a second – on a wet course at Shelsley Walsh.

Road-registered EUR 3, the Talbot-Lago was found to corner better on left-hand bends than on right; when the car was scrutineered for conformity with the regulations for the 1939 TT, which stipulated a minimum wheelbase of 8 ft 8 in for the 3–5-litre class, it was revealed that the left-hand wheelbase was 8 ft 7.5 in, while the right was 8 ft 8.5 in. . . .

In 1938, Lago offered the alternative of a 4.5-litre power unit, and it was said that in racing form this engine developed as much as 200 bhp. . . .

The road-going Talbots were bodied by such master *carrossiers* as Saoutchik and Figoni & Falaschi, the former an

BOTH PAGES Power unit of the
Talbot-Lago was designed by
Walter Becchia and derived
from the old Talbot-Darracq
3-litre engine. Launched in 4-
litre form, the engine was later
enlarged to 4.5 litres and, in
racing guise, could develop
some 200 bhp. Top speed of
this streamlined coupé would
be in the region of 140 mph

emigré Russian cabinet maker, the latter two Italians – an artist and a businessman – who were based in Boulogne-sur-Seine, close to the Bois de Boulogne and the Hippodrome de Longchamp.

Figoni had an unerring eye for flowing lines and his elegant coachwork exactly captured the mood of the moneyed set of the 1930s. Some of his creations were restrained, like the 4-litre car tested by *The Autocar* in 1939, others – like the coupé shown here – were shocking in their exuberance. 'Why, that car is positively indecent!' William Lyons of Jaguar is reported to have said on seeing this car, but it's noticeable that Lyons was not averse to copying Figoni's styling when it suited him. . . .

A supercharged 3-litre sixteen-cylinder racer was promised in 1939, but never reached fulfilment. Nor did a range of licence-built Talbot-Lagos which it was proposed to market in England under the once-great, but now moribund, Invicta name.

Tony Lago's chameleon-like persona – 'Anthony in England, Antoine in France, Antonio in Italy' – proved a godsend during the war, for it protected him from both the Germans and the French Resistance. This enabled him to get back into production very quickly after the

BOTH PAGES This rear view of the Talbot coupé (*far left*) shows the innate artistry of Figoni, for there isn't a wrong line in the entire composition; the 'Gothic arch' cross-sections of the wings were a Figoni & Falaschi hallmark. Within, the car combines function with elegance, for the instruments on the stylish dashboard (*below*) are no different from those you would expect to find on a competition car – apart from the radio!

BELOW Look at the fine detail work on the Figoni & Falaschi coupé – like this bright metal accent around the wing edges with its art nouveau overtones

Armistice with a new twin-ohc 4.5-litre power unit and a close-ratio Wilson preselector transmission. This 'Lago-Record' was the basis for both French Presidential limousines and a vast limousine for King Ibn Saud of Saudi Arabia, delivered in 1951. This long wheelbase 3-ton behemoth had full refrigeration, a lavatory, a washbasin – and over half a mile of wiring.

Some post-war Lago-Records had wondrously swoopy saloon bodywork by Saoutchik, spoiled only by an overlarge chrome radiator grille; and Figoni's 1948

show car, described as 'a visual feast from many angles', was also spoiled by its frontal aspect.

A sign of the austere times was the introduction of the 1949 'Baby' Talbot, which the catalogue described as 'a car of class with an average power output'

which the British agent described as 'awful'. Talbot sales during the 1950s were minimal; new power units — among them a Raymond Mays-converted Ford Zephyr Six and a BMW 2.5-litre V8 — were tried, but by 1960 the marque had faded away. Tony Lago died soon after.

VOISIN V12

The last survivor of Gabriel Voisin's extraordinary underslung sleeve-valve V12 cars is this 4680 cc Simoun. The daringly unconventional lines of the Simoun reveal the full flowering of Voisin's genius, influenced by his friendship with the Modernist architect Le Corbusier

There's no doubt about it: Gabriel Voisin, aesthete and insatiable womanizer, is one of the key figures in the history of transportation. One of the true pioneers of flight, he was the first man to make truly controlled flights in Europe, and was running an aeroplane factory in Paris before the Wright brothers' planes were in production.

After Voisin's factory at Issy-les-Moulineaux had built a claimed 10 000 aeroplanes, the armistice of 1918 destroyed his aviation market and he turned to car manufacture to keep his factory in business. A chassis designed by two young engineers from Panhard & Levassor named Artaud and Dufresne was acquired and put into production, its

power unit a four-cylinder double-sleeve-valve Knight engine of fractionally under 4 litres whose untapped potential for sporting performance Voisin was the first to exploit.

The first Voisin car was ready for test on 5 February 1919 – Voisin's thirty-ninth birthday – at 3am, Voisin's little team having worked into the night to finish the

prototype. But when Gabriel Voisin, seated on the upturned wooden box that served as a seat on the chassis, put the car in gear and attempted to drive off, it moved off backwards. In their haste to complete the car, Voisin's engineers had fitted the axle gearing the wrong way round!

Nevertheless, Voisin set off into the night using the one forward speed left to him – and found the asphalt road surrounding the factory covered with a thin film of ice, on which the powerful rear wheel brakes provoked quite spectacular gyrations. Now the only way for Voisin to test the gearbox before the

'I wanted exceptional flexibility, and this unattainable desire was to lead me to design a V12 engine with a capacity of 4 litres. I expected marvels of this machine. . . .'
Gabriel Voisin, 1962

rear axle was put right was to drive the chassis backwards – and he found that when he braked, instead of whizzing round like a teetotum on the ice, the prototype stopped in a straight line, every time.

'The conclusion was easy', said Voisin. 'A four-wheeled car should be braked on the front wheels!' And as soon as practicable, he put into production one of the industry's first four-wheel braked chassis, with eighty per cent of the braking effort applied to the front wheels. . . .

With production of his 18 CV four under way, Voisin, ever the inventor, let his mind wander. He owned three ancient steam cars, a Stanley, a Serpollet and a Weyher-Richemond, and loved the effortless way they gathered speed without the need for a gearbox, possessed 'shattering' (but completely silent) acceleration and could climb any slope flat out. He used parts from all three to build a modern steam car and

RIGHT
There is nothing conventional about a Voisin; when customers demanded a suitable radiator mascot, Gabriel Voisin designed the art deco 'Cocotte'. Translated, that means 'chick' or 'birdie'; it also means 'floozy'!

was again entranced, but he knew that the complication of steam was beyond the wit of the average motorist.

Translating that smooth flow of power into a post-war petrol car was less easy, but in 1920 Voisin built his first twelve-cylinder car. It was, he recalled later, an exercise in science fiction. 'The water-cooled engine was composed of three aluminium castings: the crankcase, the right-hand block of six cylinders and the left-hand block of six cylinders. All the intake and water passages, the oilways and the electrical conduits were incorporated into those castings so that nothing showed on the outside of my compact power unit. . . . The clutch was achieved by two opposed turbine wheels

LEFT So low-built was the Simoun chassis that the track rod passed well above the chassis and the axle beam arched *upwards* ... Such ground-hugging proportions were not normally attainable with rear-driven chassis

turning in oil, which could be brought to rest by an electromagnet.... There were only two forward speeds and, of course, brakes on all four wheels – but operated by compressed air...'.

The test run, from Paris to Cannes was not without incident, for the compressed-air brakes packed up and Voisin had to take an air lead from one of the engine's cylinders to power them. Then something seized in the turbine clutch which Voisin tried to free by squirting petrol into the casing with a syringe. Unfortunately, the drive shaft was so hot that the petrol vaporized and exploded, sending a shower of very warm, very black oil over him. ...

A couple of rest days in Cannes permitted the necessary repairs and the V12 made the return journey of just over 600 miles in 16 hr 35 min: it would be difficult to cover the same distance at an average of over 37 mph even today. The V12 had one major failing: that 'science fiction' specification was horrendously expensive and it just wasn't practicable to put it into production, although many of its mechanical features found their way on to the 'normal' Voisins (among whose dedicated owners was Rudolph Valentino, who bought a tourer for himself and a brougham for his wife Natacha Rambova).

Voisin didn't abandon his dream of putting a twelve-cylinder car into production: it was, he admitted, one of his pet obsessions, along with aerodynamic design and an unfulfilled desire to build the world's fastest car. Late in 1929, a twelve-cylinder Voisin racer appeared at the Montlhéry track near Paris, and broke a series of endurance records up to 20 000 km before crashing. In the wake of this achievement, Gabriel Voisin introduced the Diane, a 3860 cc V12 luxury car of quite remarkable design, with a crankshaft virtually 4 inches in diameter and all twenty-four sleeves driven from a single eccentric shaft set between the two banks of cylinders and – for a V12 – of simple construction. 'Repairs and adjustments can be carried out by any skilled workman,' claimed Voisin, 'even if his training has been limited to dealing with poppet-valve engines.'

Lightness of the reciprocating parts was rigorously pursued and Voisin said that the engine could run at a steady 4000 rpm, although, he added with typical contempt for his average customer: 'In the hands of drivers who refuse to show any discretion or forethought, and who are acquainted only with the fully depressed accelerator position, sleeves will occasionally seize. Usually this is

RIGHT Voisin provided his V12 cars with an electromagnetically engaged overdrive on all three speeds; purist that he was, he provided no covering for the transmission housing but left it exposed in the centre of the passenger compartment

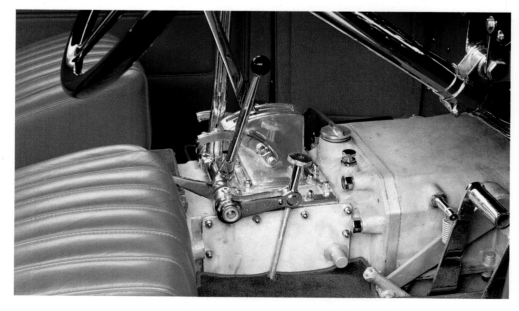

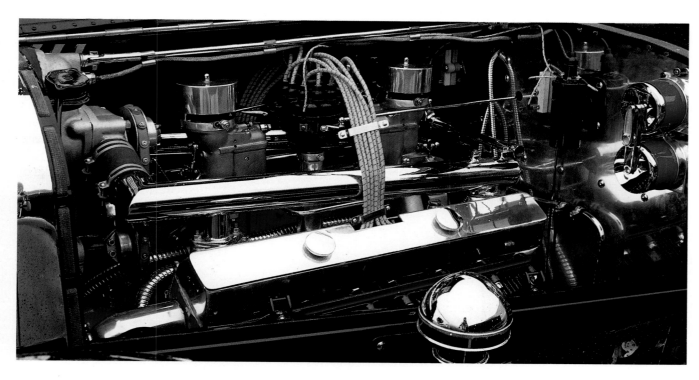

disastrous for the entire engine, but with the Voisin design there is a safety device whereby the seized sleeve remains in the cylinder. Although, of course, it will have to be replaced, the damage is limited to this renewal.'

Motoring journalist W.F. Bradley remarked that the 115 bhp power unit gave 'a flexibility as to performance comparable with that of a steamer'. Nevertheless, the Diane had an electomagnetically operated overdrive on all speeds, giving the choice of six speeds forward and two reverse: either side of the propeller shaft lay long petrol tanks giving sufficient capacity for a range of 300 miles, while in the position behind the back axle normally occupied by the fuel tank was a locker holding the tools and twin batteries.

'As the useful load is carried between the axles,' noted Bradley, 'it makes little difference to the balance of the car whether it consists of one or six persons'.

Balance was an important concept to Gabriel Voisin, and in 1930, the Diane was joined by the astounding Sirocco, a remarkably low-slung sports saloon with a 5830 cc V12 engine; the Simoun was similar, but with a 4860 cc power unit which was also available as an option in the Diane.

The underslung chassis had axles inverted above the springs, which were carried in raised brackets to give the Sirocco truly ground-hugging proportions; claimed top speed was 95 mph – a remarkable figure indeed for a sleeve-valve car.

Voisin built few Siroccos or Simouns – these were, after all, the years of the Great Depression – but he wasn't finished with his twelve-cylinder hobbyhorse: 'For my personal use,' he later recalled, 'I built an aerosport car powered by twelve cylinders *in line* . . . of course the engine came back under the scuttle, but that was no worse than the little "mountain" inflicted on the front seat passengers by the transmission tunnel . . . the engine capacity of this phenomenon was 5 litres and it developed 150 bhp at 3000 rpm; two-up, it was timed at 106 mph at Montlhéry. . .'.

Voisin's visions were too pure to make commercial sense, and even he was

ABOVE Claiming that the Voisin V12 could rotate at a constant 4000 rpm, Gabriel Voisin nevertheless provided the engine with a safety device which prevented seized sleeves from damaging the engine

'One man's meat is another man's poisin,' wrote motoring poet W.H. Charnock. 'But my favourite car is an Avions Voisin . . .'

forced to admit that his company's finances were 'hardly brilliant' at the time of the V12 venture. The inevitable happened, and financiers took control of the company. They compelled Voisin to produce a car powered not by his beloved sleeve-valves but by a pedestrian side-valve engine from an American Graham. Voisin's opinion of this machine

is encapsulated in the code name of the chassis: 'Brick'. . . .

He wasn't finished with cars; after the war he designed the sub-utility 125 cc Biscooter, of which some 18 000 were sold in Spain, but it was the fantastic underslung Sirocco and Simoun which were the high points of his unique career as a motor manufacturer. By any

standards, production was minute – Voisin's claim of eighty-two V12 cars built in total was almost certainly exaggeration – and today only one of the underslung V12s survives, a Simoun preserved in the Blackhawk Collection in California.

Voisin, who lived to the age of ninety-three, had little time for the cars of his past, and once told a collector who owned a vintage Voisin: 'It is difficult for me to understand the reasons which compel you to utilize some absolute junk with no practical value when modern industry places mechanical marvels at your disposal. . . . I advise you to find some imbecile, sell him your Voisin, and with the proceeds of the sale get yourself an English Mini. . .'.

INDEX

Page numbers in *italic* refer to illustrations

Alfa Romeo 11, 14, 15, 18, 22, 24, 88, 187, 191
Astaire, Fred 215
Aston Martin 28, 30, 31, 118, 119
Austin Healey 112
Alfonso XIII 53, 128
AVUS 186

Baker, Josephine 84
Baracca Francesco *15*
Barnato, Woolf 35, 38
Becchia, Walter 224, 227
Benjafield, Dudley 35, 36
Benoist, Robert 67
Bentley 35–9
Bentley, W.O. 36, 51, 75
Birkigt, Marc 128, 139
Birkin, Tim 35, 37, 39
Bizzarrini, Giotto 112
Blackhawk Collection 132, 143, 239
Bohman & Schwartz *103*
Bradley, W.F. 51, 237
Brooklands 24, *39*, 88
Brooks, Tony 28
Boris, King of Albania 53
Brauchitsch, Manfred von 187
Bucciali 42, 43, 46, 47
Bucciali, Angelo 42
Bucciali, Paul Albert 42, 43, *49*
Buehrig, Gordon 102
Bugatti, Ettore 51, 52, *52*, 54, 58, 67, 134
Bugatti 50–67, 134, 139
Bugatti, Jean 52, 58, *59*, 62, 64, 65
Bugatti, Rembrandt 54, *54*

Cadillac 68, 69, 70, 74, 75
Campbell, Malcolm 182, 184
Castagna *143*, 147, 149
Caproni, Giovanni 147
Carol, King of Romania 53
Cattaneo, Giustino 143, 146
Causan, Nemorin 79
Chapron 90
Charbonneaux, Phillipe *56*, 90
Charnock, W.H. 238
Chiti, Carlo 117
Citroën, André 53
Clement Talbot 224
Colombo, Cioacchino 111
Clark, Jim 112
Cooper, Gary 106, 108
Cord, Erret Loban 46, 102
Costatini, Bartolomeo 62
Crane Simplex 201
Crook, Anthony 21, 22
Cunningham, Briggs 51, 54
Cutting, Ted 26, 31

Daimler, Gottlieb 164, 173
Daimler, Paul 180
Darracq 88
Davis, S.C.H. 36, 37
De Dion-Bouton 79
Delage, Louis 79, 83
Delahaye 24, 84, 85, 87, 90, *94*, 97
Delling, Erik, H. 201
Dempsey, Jack 146
Dietrich, Ray *208*
Dreyfuss, René 64, 94
Dubonnet, Andre 132
Duesenberg 100–2, 106–8
Duesenberg, August 100
Duesenberg, Fred S. 102
Duff, John 36, 38

Earl, Harley 74
Etancelin, Phillipe 39

Fairbanks, Douglas 143
Farina 25, 147
Faroux, Charles, 134
Ferrari 14, 15, 111, 112, 116, 123, 124, 156
Ferrari, Enzo 11, 111, 116, 124
Figoni & Falaschi 65, *85*, 90, *100*, 226, 230
Flockhart, Ron 153
Ford, Henry 218
Foulkes-Halbard, Paul *11*, *177*, *177*
Franay 65, 97
Fraschini, Oreste 146
Frère, Paul 28

Gable, Clark 103, 106, *107*, 108
Gangloff 64
Gardner, Goldie *11*, 15
Gaultier, Maurice 79, 83
Gauntlett, Victor 26, 30, 31, *32*
Gendebien, Olivier 118, 119
Ghia 147
Goering, Herman 192
Graber 65
Gurney, Dan 116
Gurney Nutting 38, 65
Guynemer, Georges 132, *132*

Hamilton, Duncan *151*
Harrah, William 47, 53
Hawthorn, Mike 119, 151, 153
Hearst, Randolph 107, 143
Hill, Graham 112
Hill, Phil 116, 119, 125
Hispano-Suiza *49*, 83, 128, 133, 134, 138, 139, 146
Horch 168
Hotchkiss 90
Hughes, Howard 107

Iaccoca, Lee 123
Ickx, Jacky 127
Isotta Fraschini *143*, 147

Jaguar 150–4, 156, 229
Jano, Vittorio 11
Jaray, Paul 22, 168
Jellinek, Emil 172
Jenatzy, Camille 176
Jenkins, Ab 211
Johnson, Claude 219, 220

Kent, Prince Michael of 32

Labourdette 65
Lago, Antonio 224, 229, 231
Lampredi, Aurelio 111
Letourner & Marchand 65, *80*, 84, 90
Levegh, Pierre 112
Lister Jaguar 28
Lombard, Carole 103
Lunn, Roy 125
Lyons, William 224, 229, *231*

Macklin, Lance 112, 153
Marek, Tadek 26, *29*
Maybach 164, 167–9
Maybach, Karl 164
Maybach, Wilhelm 173
Mays, Raymond 231
Mercer 196, 199, 201
Mercedes 94, 112, 152, 169, 172–6, 180, 185, 188, 192, *192*
Milton, Tommy 207
Mille Miglia 12, 16, 21, 22, 25, 32, 94, 96, 186
Monte Carlo Rally 86, 88
Moss, Stirling 28, 31, 212
Mussolini, Benito 15
McLaren, Bruce 125
McQueen, Steve *152*, 155, 156

Nacker, Owen 70
Nibel, Hans 192
Nuvolari, Tazio *11*, 12, 13, 16

Olley, Maurice 74

Packard 69, 204–8, 215, 216
Paget, Dorothy 37
Panhard & Levassor 232
Pintacuda, Carlo 21
Pierce Arrow 212, 216, 217
Porsche, Ferdinand 181, 182

Rainier, Prince 97
Rivers-Fletcher A.F. 38
Roebling, C.G. 196
Roebling, Washington 196
Rolls-Royce 100, 146, 208, 219, 220, 221
Rolls, Charles Stewart 219
Roosevelt, Franklin D. 208
Royce, Henry 218, *221*

Sailer, Max 192
Sala, Cesare 147

Salvadori, Roy 28, 31
Saoutchik, Jacques *43*, 48, 62, 65, 138, 168, 226
Saud, King Ibn of Arabia 230
Sayer, Malcolm 152
Scott-Brown, Archie 28
Seaholm, Ernest 70
Shelby, Carroll 125
Sommer, Raymond *18*, 25, 67
Studebaker 211, 216
Surtees, John 112

Targa Florio 12, 118, 120, 128, 132
Tjaarda, John 216
Trintignant, Maurice 118
Trips, Wolfgang von 116
Turgan–Foy 79

Valentino, Rudolf 143, 236
Van den Plas 38
Van Vooren 65
Villiers, Amherst 37
Vincent, Jesse G. 204
Voisin 48, 236–9
Voisin, Gabriel 83, 97, 232, 233, *234*, 237

West, Mae 106
Walker, Rob 24, 90, 112
Weiffenbach, Charles 86
Weymann, C.T. 52
Whitehead, Graham 26, 28
Whitehead, Peter 26, 28
Wimille, Jean-Paul 67
Wright, Philip 215, 216
Wyer, John 26, 31

Young, James 64

Zagato 11, *17*, 30
Zborowski, Count Eliot 175
Zog, King of Albania 182